T0285837

BIS Publishers
Borneostraat 80-A
1094 CP Amsterdam
The Netherlands
T +31 (0)20 515 02 30
bis@bispublishers.com
www.bispublishers.com

ISBN 978 90 636 9648 1

Copyright © 2022 Aga Szóstek and BIS Publishers.

Copyedited by Diane Parker.

Graphic & Layout by Dominika Wysogląd.

Layout by Agnieszka Gontarz.

Illustrations by Weronika Marianna.

All rights reserved. No part of this publication may be reproduced
or transmitted in any form or by any means, electronic or mechanical,
including photocopy, recording or any information storage and retrieval
system, without permission in writing from the copyright owners.

Every reasonable attempt has been made to identify owners
of copyright. Any errors or omissions brought to the publisher's
attention will be corrected in subsequent editions.

Aga Szóstek, PhD

Leadership by Design

The essential guide to transforming you as a leader

For Łukasz
– it will forever fascinate me
how your brain works.

For Maja and Kacper
– I hope you will never cease to occupy
the driving seat of your lives.

For Dominika, Weronika and Agnieszka
– the design dream team.

In loving memory of Maddy Janse
– the director of the User System Interaction programme
at Eindhoven University of Technology
who gave me the most important
wild card of my professional life.

List Of Contents

Foreword

In my first job within Canon, I led a team of ten engineers, along with my technical lead Dom. Dom found me helping some of the engineers write software, and asked me to stop doing that. "I have another nine people who can write software", he said, "but you're the only one who can lead." That was the start of my realisation as to what value I can add as a leader.

I now manage Canon Medical's Healthcare IT Engineering with over 500 engineers building medical device software across seven R&D centres around the world. I've learned how to lead across cultures, across functions, and to lead with influence alone when needed. There have been many transitions in my leadership role in my career, and with few exceptions, I've had to learn to manage those transitions myself.

Over the years, I've read a lot of leadership books — most of them written by business leaders, military leaders, or sports coaches who tell you what they did to succeed. I've learned slowly and painfully that copying another leader's style is unlikely to translate well to a different type of organisation, or to a different culture. You have to find your own approach.

If I'd had *Leadership by Design* when I started working with Dom, I would have understood the transition I should have been taking, from contributor to leader. If I had it later in my career, it would have helped me find my way in managing across functions, or in knowing my personal leadership values when faced with challenges. When circumstances mean you need to lay off some staff, dramatically change what people are working on, or untangle conflicts between staff — having a deep understanding of who you are as a leader can make it much easier to find a way to be genuine and human when you do so.

I feel that the best leadership books are written by those who study leaders as journalists or academics. Next to being a designer, Aga is a researcher, and an expert observer. She has been working with leaders on every level, from team leads to CEOs, helping them bring an experience strategy into their organisations. All that expertise was captured in her previous book, the Umami Strategy. By working with so many leaders she learned that to bring strategy into an organisation from outside, you have to deeply understand what leadership is about.

Aga and I first discussed leadership in a little bar in Warsaw, after the Agile by Example conference, which she was a fellow speaker at. To talk to Aga about your leadership experience is to find yourself talking about how you lead, and why you lead in that way, but also about how you learned what you do. She draws stories from you, and synthesises any small wisdom you might offer with that she's drawn from others.

From her observations, and the deep pool of rich ideas gathered during the Catching the Next Wave podcast, Aga pulls together knowledge and assembles a series of learning steps that you can use to find your own way of leading, and design your path to achieving it. It's about appreciating that no leadership style is ever perfect, and learning to lead is a continual and evolving process. She finds the balanced path between provoking you to thoughts and feelings about leadership, and allowing you enough comfort to keep following and working through the exercises.

If you're a leader who seeks to lead by influence rather than authority: maybe because you're transitioning to a more senior role, or because you're a freelancer, or a community leader, then this book will help you find a process for continually improving your leadership practice. It offers a path to becoming a softer, more balanced and humanistic leader than most books will offer you. And I believe that is where the future of leadership lies.

Malcolm Campbell
Global VP of Engineering
Canon Medical, Healthcare IT

Introduction

Leadership practice

Resistance

What will happen as you keep on going?

To be a good leader for others
you must be able to lead yourself first.

Rob van der Tillaart

I have never done it before
so I think I can do it.

Pippi Longstocking

eo Tolstoy famously begins his novel *Anna Karenina* with the sentence, "Happy families are all alike, every unhappy family is unhappy in its own way".[1] These words can be easily transposed onto each and every organisation in the world. So far, though I've encountered quite a few happy families, I have yet to encounter a perfectly happy organisation. This is not to say that happy organisations don't exist. I would guess, however, that they are rarer than Bengal tigers or blue moons. Happy organisations are so rare because they are made up of people with their personalities, quirks, needs, dreams, fears and, above all, expectations.* This is the reason why entirely happy organisations (and, by a happy organisation, I mean one where every person in it feels happy) are, frankly, a utopian mirage, aren't they?

When I first became a leader, I thought that there was an optimal way of leading. So, I kept on looking for the perfect leadership model. It turned out there wasn't one — at least, not for me. As a result, I decided that perhaps I wasn't leadership material after all. I saw my friends and colleagues battling the same challenge. There seemed to be a prevalent conviction among us that there was a leadership ideal and we all should strive to reach it. The cost of doing so was often high: loneliness, burnout, depression, you name it. Was that really the price to pay for becoming a leader, I wondered? Or was there something very wrong with the way we approached leadership development?

In recent years, I have worked with various leaders on defining the experience strategy for their solutions and brands, which I describe in *The Umami Strategy*. After discovering how a great experience strategy helped their customers become better versions of themselves, many of these leaders asked whether they could undergo

* This is what a leader needs to consider every day

a similar transformation in the way they lead. So, I found myself once again trying to capture what great leadership was all about. This exploration showed me that, much as with experience design, there is no one way, one recipe, one silver-bullet piece of advice. I realised that becoming a great leader meant coming to terms with yourself, your family, your team, your peers and your superiors while facing your beliefs, understanding your purpose and respecting who you are as a unique human being. To aid those leaders, I prepared for them a reflection journal full of questions and exercises. After seeing how well the journal worked, the initial idea for this book was born. But how to write a book about leadership when there are so many out there already?

Leadership practice

After I had finished writing *The Umami Strategy*, I felt creatively drained and I found myself in a rather dark place; one that could be best compared to what mothers of newborn children often experience as 'baby blues'. At the same time, I felt both bursting with the content for this book and scared to write it. So many people, after all, say that everybody has one book in them, but only a very few are able to write the second one, or the third. This is why I decided to reach for a book that had been sitting on my shelf waiting for me for over five years, Julia Cameron's *The Artist's Way*[2]. For those of you who may not be familiar with it, this book is a twelve-week course in discovering and recovering your creativity. It is divided into twelve chapters with creative exercises and some challenging questions at the end of each chapter. As I was working through that course, it dawned on me that this is exactly how I would love to write my leadership book — not as a recipe but as a collection of reflections and exercises that allows you, as a reader, to discover your own leadership practice, much like the early explorers discovered new lands.

This is why this book is designed as a twelve-week course. It is based on the premise that the way to define your leadership practice is to have an open, honest conversation with yourself; a conversation that will hopefully continue long into the future. The consecutive weeks will challenge your perspectives and make you reconsider and reshape them, in a gentle yet persistent manner. You will defy your expectations of what it means to be a leader and shift your views into new directions to explore what fits you best. It will help you to stop trying to fit into the leadership vision that others might have about you, and help you learn to stay flexible while continuously defining what leadership style fits you in a given and ever-changing context.

Resistance

This book is your personal transformation guide. Such transformation needs to be challenging to make it stick. It requires your (full) commitment and stamina. It might feel scary. Most likely, you will experience mental blockage, discouragement and the urge to return to the status quo. These are all the symptoms of Resistance (with a capital 'R'). The concept of Resistance is beautifully described in *The War of Art*.[3]. Its author, Steven Pressfield, argues that Resistance is a powerful force that keeps you from reaching your potential. It is a force that makes you follow the path of, well, the least resistance. Resistance keeps you focused on short-term goals, instant gratification and immediate pleasure. It loathes long-term thinking, commitment and radical change. It encourages you to keep on doing more of the same and discourages you from choosing to do something different. In other words, Resistance will push you to follow what's known and established. It will make you hold on to the status quo. The more you try to transform, the stronger Resistance will be — from your friends, your team, your peers, your bosses, and other (external and internal) agents that lobby against that change. They will often do whatever is in their power to keep you on the 'safe track', to make you do more of the same. But the biggest Resistance will be that which comes from yourself, from that little critic inside your head whispering in your ear that you cannot do it. It may take the form of mental blockage, annoyance, anger, discouragement and sometimes failure; even the desire to abandon the journey altogether.

It is crucial to bear in mind that Resistance is nothing more than your personal self-sabotaging mechanism, something that you say to yourself to stop you from becoming the leader you want to be. It feeds on the expectations we and others have of ourselves, turning them into the stories we live by. It may be that you will think:
- 'I am too old for that'.
- 'I am too young for that'.
- 'I will never be as good as...'.
- 'I will never be able to change my ways'.

I imagine Resistance as monkeys in my head that feed on drama and conflict. Resolving the conflicts and cooling off the dramas gives an impression of change. But extinguishing fires is not progress. In order to combat Resistance, you need to get to know your expectations (which is not an easy job in the least) and then reshape them in new ways.

What will happen as you keep on going?

Consider this: we replace every cell in our body every three years. Our memory is flexible and re-formattable. So, every one of us has the power to, as Gandhi once said, "become the change you want to see in the world". After you are done with this book, you are not going to be the person you are today. We change and transform in our lives regardless, whether we use any aids to do so or not. So, why not to turn such transformation into a conscious and deliberate process? In a way, you are setting yourself up for an adventure deep within yourself, with this book as your map.

Every adventure has a few characteristics. For once, you don't know what is going to happen, so you can't quite prepare yourself. Also, there will be adversity and difficulty along the way — otherwise, it wouldn't be an adventure. Once you start changing, many of the old ways will stop working and you need to be mindful of that. You will most likely feel tired, even discouraged. But you will also feel exhilarated and energised.

Some of the ideas captured in these pages may inspire you, some may be... meh... It is because this adventure is a deeply personal one, and you will naturally pay attention to the things that are important to you at that moment. Actually, if you choose to re-read this book at a different time, different elements of it are likely to catch your interest and be a catalyst for reflection and further change.

At the end of this adventure, you will have developed a better sense of self-understanding, a stronger and more clear sense of self. You will have plenty of new leadership practice, ways of behaving, routines, a communication style that fits who you are. You will also find a stronger peace of mind regarding the way you resonate with the world, with your organisation and with yourself. It may also happen that you decide that leadership is not for you. If you arrive at such a conclusion, consider it as a catalyst to get you on the path of realising your full potential. Such a discovery is not a failure in any sense. It is a sign that you are ready to listen to your deep self and follow its wisdom.

Above all, this book is in no way a prescription of what leadership should be. It is a personal practice and, hopefully, a great journey. Each week will provoke you to think about the different challenges leaders face on their path. This selection is neither finite nor definitive, but I hope it touches upon the aspects of leadership that are crucial for you too.

Although this course can be undertaken alone, you might consider inviting others to join you: your accountability buddies.*, 4 Although you may be perfectly capable of following through without external help, a transformational process is often more effective when you have support. "Some people are very accountable to themselves, but not most people", said Dr Tim Church, a chief medical officer for Naturally Slim, an application-based behavioural health program in Dallas. "In my years of working with thousands of people, there's one thing that drives accountability more than anything else: If you want to keep people doing a behaviour, get a buddy."5 You can create such accountability by checking in with a friend, or, even better, having someone follow this course alongside you. Accountability might mean arranging a 'synchro session' every week or planning a daily check-in to see how you each are doing. It gives you the gentle feeling of friendly peer-pressure, focused on mutual encouragement, support and, above all, a celebration of your successes.

Finally, you might be asking yourself whether this book is for you. You don't have to be in an official position as 'leader' to benefit from going through this process. First, we lead ourselves, then our relationships, work and communities. Even if you are not part of an official organisational hierarchy, you might have been (silently and subconsciously) chosen by your peers to lead.

The goal of this course is to help you find the leadership practice that is natural to you and that makes you feel fulfilled in your role — whatever that may be. Such practice is crucial because it will help you spot old habits you are holding onto and then figure out ways in which you can alter them so they are a better fit for your own needs and those of the people around you. It is in fact an exercise in leaving the status quo behind. Because in order to embrace something new, something old needs to be abandoned.

---

* Gretchen Rubin, the author of Better than Before, says that accountability is an important tool for making and breaking habits.

Getting Started

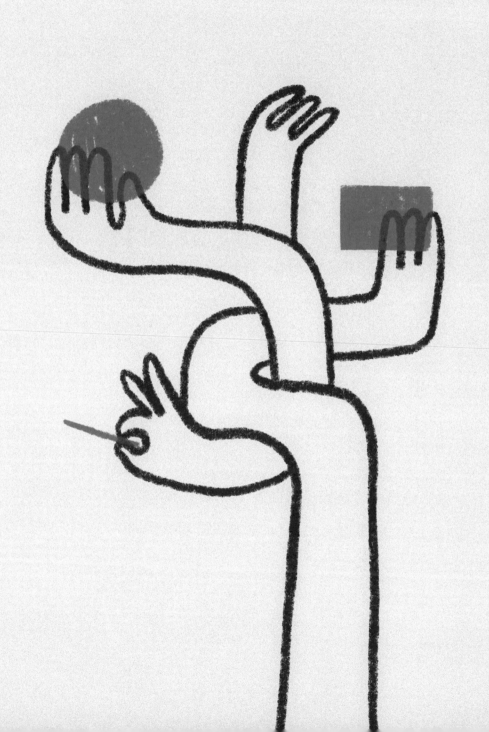

*Many organisations and communities have a technological
debt, and they also have a leadership debt. When you join
a new institution, you are presented with an implicit
and undefined set of assumptions on how to lead.
I guess it is an amalgamation of the ghosts of the past
and present leaders, with their good and bad habits amplified
by the general organisational culture. So, it is safe to assume
that there is no single answer to the question of what
'good' leadership is in a place you find yourself. Any answer
you come up with is a good one as long as you feel
that your approach suits you and helps others around you
develop their potential. You probably already have
a sense of what you appreciate about the leaders,
supervisors and managers you met on your path so far
and what you want to avoid at any cost.*

H ave you noticed that, once you embark on a leadership track, you need to learn so many things from scratch? You might have already taken leadership courses and learned tools for project and priorities management, finances and even some soft skills such as people management. You might have tried to apply some of the leadership frameworks available out there. These courses and models too often act like strait-jackets. They keep you tight and uncomfortable, and make you question your own sanity as a person and as a leader. There is a lot of merit in them, of course; but, they miss out on the fact that, above all, leadership means being deeply human. And no human is fully shaped by a framework or made an expert with a help of a tool. What makes us grow and develop is looking inside ourselves, trying out things: failing — and learning.

Despite what I just wrote, there is somehow a prevalent notion that an ideal leadership style exists. It's not only a belief about leadership, actually. We seem to believe that we could be ideal parents, ideal partners, ideal community members. Yet, you don't become a great parent because you read a parenting book and you 'understand how that works', 'get the rules' and 'apply the ultimate parenting model'. You become a great parent once you realise that your children are unique, different from each other and yourself, and your relationship with them is something that is created by both you and them, in iterations, by listening and reflecting on what worked and what didn't. It's the same with leadership: unless you discover how to be a leader as yourself — true to yourself, aware of your values, fears, hopes and your own resistance — you will only ever be *acting* as a leader, instead of *being* one.

Are the leadership models uselful then?

Certainly, the different leadership models available in business and academic literature offer immense knowledge and inspiration. But these models are not meant to be lived by.* We humans are both complex and unique, and assuming that any one model could describe all our quirks and idiosyncrasies is not very believable, is it? This doesn't mean you should reject them all. They are great at pinpointing certain elements that might be considered important from one perspective or another. But it is important to bear in mind that not one model offers a complete representation of any single person.** After all, you are dynamic in many dimensions, not a frozen identity like a persona. This is why you most likely fit into more than one model at any one time or be a representation of one model in one context and of a completely different one in another. It is particularly important to bear in mind that our context defines the boundaries of what is possible and what is not, which strategies are likely to be successful and which will most certainly be a complete failure. If you change your context, your leadership style will likely need to adapt too. On the top of it, you will also change as a person over time and under the, often invisible, influence of the people who surround you. Thus, whatever leadership practice you create for yourself, will evolve as you develop and as your context alters. This practice will, in turn, stimulate you to grow and alter the context in which you work.***

---

*   There should be a warning sign on them much like on a pack of cigarettes.

**   I must admit the fault partially lies with the academic community. We academics love to reduce the complexity of the world and people, and try to translate it into graspable models.

***   If you ask various leaders and leadership experts how they define leadership, they will most likely tell you that you need to create your own definition. Coming up with such a definition requires you to investigate for yourself what skills and competencies are the core ingredients of a good leadership practice. If such leadership definition does not come from within, you are not going to own it. In other words, the only leadership practice that will fit you is the one you create yourself.

The process of defining your own leadership practice begins by you imagining the situation you are hoping to find yourself in.* I am a fan of a quote by Frank Underwood: "imagination is its own form of courage".[6] Imagination helps you to dream big about your potential and create scenarios in which this potential can be realised. Imagination enables you to adapt to the changing context and expands your creativity in seeking new ways of being and acting as a leader.**

Design-inspired approach

When conducting research for my first book *The Umami Strategy*, I tried to understand how people create narratives about their own lives. The person I turned to for such wisdom is one of the most cited psychologists of the present day, Lisa Feldman Barrett, who shows how the story we tell ourselves about who we are defines who we become.[7] There are two assumptions here — the first is that we have an image of who we would like to become and the second is that we have the tools that will help us get there. This is where the design process comes into play. It consists of four elements: better understanding the context you find yourself in; creating alternative approaches to stimulate the desired change; testing these approaches and analysing their outcomes to; finally, choosing the most promising one. It also offers you ways to iterate your solutions and adapt them over time, and in that way endlessly continue to develop who you are as a leader.

Being a designer, these processes are my daily bread and butter but I guess they may not be so for you, so let's talk for a moment about how it all works. Every design process begins by knowing very little to nothing. Sometimes we, as designers, fall under the misconception that we know stuff but more often than not, this is not true at all. So, step one of any such project is to get to know our stakeholders, their problems,

---

*   As the Nobel laureate Herbert Simon said about design, "To design is to devise courses of action aimed at changing existing situations into preferred ones".

**   A Russian psychologist, Lev Vygotsky, wrote that our brain, "constantly combines and creatively reworks elements of past experience and uses them to generate new propositions and new behaviour. It is precisely human creative activity that makes the human being a creature oriented towards the future, creating the future and thus altering their own present".

needs, desires and dreams. Gaining that knowledge allows us to envision a better future, which our solution helps to achieve. However, as humans we are not very good at figuring out the consequences of our design decisions (both intended and unintended) so designers typically use two tools to mitigate that. We often create more than one idea to enable the stakeholders to explore alternative directions towards the final solution. I am, personally, a fan of creating three different concepts for what I am designing — a conservative one, a crazy one and something in the middle. In that way, I can see how far I can go with my imagination to achieve the result I am hoping for and the stakeholders are willing to accept.* Then we test those ideas in the wild, so, in other words, we experiment by confronting our stakeholders with the concepts we created to see what works and what doesn't.

Let's transpose this process onto that in which you are about to engage yourself. The first challenge lies in the fact that you wish to (re)design *yourself* as a leader, so you are your own most important stakeholder. You need to investigate your challenges, needs, desires and dreams to understand what your leadership practice is today and how you want to evolve it over time.** Once you get to understand your needs, it will be time for defining concepts, creating experiments

---

*   Why would we need alternative concepts? As humans, we are not too good at abstract thinking. If I showed you a pen and asked you what you think about it, you might describe its colour, length and maybe its writing qualities, if you got a chance to write a few words with it. But if I show you two pens, things become infinitely more interesting. You immediately start having opinions about the first and the second pen that you like and dislike. Most likely in the end you may not choose one pen or the other but create an amalgamation of those two pens that define the third ideal pen for you. Similarly with testing design solutions, if I show you just one concept, you may correct some details about it but I will know little about your actual preferences. If I present two or three different concepts for you to compare against each other, I will end up with a combination of design propositions, creating a fourth solution that most likely substantially better fits the problem at hand. I can then iterate my concept to improve the solution even further.

**   In other words, this exercise of leadership design can be seen as tailoring a suit. If it does not fit, you won't wear it. The suit is yours, it's personal. The longer you wear such a suit, it fits better and better. Did you ever buy a second-hand suit? It always feels like someone already inhabits it.

and testing them out in real life with your other stakeholders — your peers, your team, your bosses.

It is crucial to remember that the design approach is just an approach within which you act. What you put into this exercise will determine the quality of the output. It is not about 'making the moves', it is about doing hard cognitive and emotional labour to comprehend the change you want to see and then deducing how this change can be created, while keeping an eye on the unexpected consequences that will appear sooner or later. When they do, you will need to adjust your course through another set of experiments to find a way of maintaining your desired change. You may also find yourself redefining what the 'desired change' is in the first place, so not only your path may alter but also the destination. I've seen this happen with many leaders. They believed in one approach to leading their teams only to find out that another approach was much more beneficial to themselves and others. It takes guts to notice that and even more guts to follow through with the change while letting go of several practices that might have served you in the past but no longer do so.

There is one core difference between design projects and designing your own leadership style worthwhile mentioning here. During the design process, designers make many assumptions at once so the change they want to achieve is readily visible once the final concept is created. You are entering a less radical process. Each week will be one iteration of a small number of elements of your leadership practice. Imagine building a tower of LEGO blocks from behind a curtain. You can add, replace or remove blocks and you can feel the shape changing but the final result will most likely be nothing like you imagine along the way. For this, you need to become equipped with two tools: reflective practice and experimentation.

Reflective practice

Professor Lisa Feldman Barrett says that emotions we experience are appropriations that our brain constructs in a moment in anticipation of what might happen next.[8] She points out that our brain doesn't react to the world as such, but it predicts and constructs our life experience. A piece of knowledge acquired a moment ago changes how we perceive

an ongoing chain of events. In other words, our emotions are the building blocks for the stories we tell ourselves. Whenever we hope for a transformational experience to land with us, we need to have the time and
the space to integrate the thoughts we have on how and who we want
to be in the world through a process called *metacognition*. Reflection is
exactly that, a way of integrating your observations and gleaning from
these the conclusions for your daily practice.

I imagine that you are a busy person and it may not always be possible for you to spend time reflecting every day. However, try to do so as
often as possible. In writing. Get yourself a great notebook, something
that will inspire you to write in it. Keep it close as a reminder of your
commitment. Write longhand rather than on your computer to slow
down your thoughts and give yourself more space to spot what you may
not otherwise notice. The best moment to do so is either in the morning,
before you get pulled into the day's challenges, or in the evening, after
everything has stopped (for a moment at least). Use the tasks you will
find at the end of each chapter to guide your thinking. They are divided
into core tasks and extras. The core tasks aim to cover the key points
tackled during each week. The extras are there if you would like to dig
deeper and challenge yourself further.

Remember that your notes are for you and you alone. This notebook
is your tool to notice what you usually miss out on and a way to see what
it is possible to change. Set aside about two hours weekly to go through
the exercises (it is only twenty minutes per day — I hope you can spare
that much). Make it your «me time», your little mental gym, where you
stretch and build on your current preconceptions of leadership. You will
be surprised how far and deep in your thinking such reflective practice
can take you.

The secret power of experimentation

A leader once told me that she was afraid. Her team was working on a project and the vision for the project was taking them into uncharted territory.
They sensed it was a good direction but it was not a direction they had
ever explored before. After some discussion, it appeared that the tension was that of the status quo. The team wanted to propose a solution

that would change the way they worked. Their boss did not want to change anything. Suddenly my friend found herself facing a choice: either to conform or to follow her heart. The scary part of following her heart rested on the realisation that she was unable to say if her heart was right. Resistance raised its head, sensing an opportunity to bite. Her team started dwelling on the decision, trying to go back, yet unable to give up their idea. The tension grew and she felt torn about what to do.

"When was the last time that you did something for the first time?", I asked her.[9] She recalled a change she had introduced a week earlier. As she told me that story, I could see a realisation in her eyes. A realisation that if she did something new, fear was part of the deal. Even more, fear was an indication that you were onto something you've never done before: something that could be a flop or a great success. Knowing that changing your ways can feel scary is an important realisation and also a mantra saying that without fear there is no learning, no progress, no growth. No guts, no glory. At the same time it becomes clear that when you are doing something for the first time, going all in is not the best strategy either. You would be wise to figure out first whether your new approach has a chance of success. Fortunately, there is a great tool that helps with this — experimentation.

Any experiment should begin by setting a hypothesis or, in other words, an assumption of what change you expect to see as a result of it. For example, if you decide you are going to compliment your team more on their hard work, your hypothesis for such a change might be that they will work harder and get more satisfaction out of work. Now you can test your assumptions and see whether they are valid or not.

Experiments should have a clear end point. Give yourself a short, finite time to see whether your hypothesis proves true or false. If you set a deadline in a year's time, for example, there might be so many other factors that will impact on this experiment that you won't be sure whether it worked or not. A good time stretch would be one week, perhaps two, maybe a month but no longer. Limited time frame is important for another reason — the lightness of your commitment. If you commit yourself to a year-long experiment, whatever practice you try out will most likely become your default practice. But if your commitment is for only a week or two, most people won't even notice the change so if it doesn't work, you can stop it with little or no consequences.[*]

Finally, you need to consider upfront what failure or success mean to you. Let's look again at the example experiment I mentioned earlier, offering more praise to your team. A failure may mean that nothing changes, no matter what you say.[**] That's fairly simple (or it may seem so because it would be worthwhile to figure out the underlying reason for lack of any reaction). But what is a success criterion? It could be delivering more work in a week, or perhaps a change in the atmosphere at the office. How can you 'measure' that then?

This is where intuition comes into play. Thinking that you need to base your judgments on intuition might feel, well, unintuitive, especially if you generally try to make decisions based on reason and logic. Yet, at the end of the day every decision we make is made intuitively.[10] Trusting your gut means that you believe in your own expertise as a leader to assess the change you see once you understand what change you are seeking.[***]

---

[*]   There is one more benefit of a short timeframe. Imagine that you set that yearly deadline for yourself. The change you might try to plan for is likely to be quite significant. Resistance will do everything in its power to stop you from changing that much. A weekly experiment allows you to take small steps, introducing little changes over and over again, helping you to learn quickly in small, resistance-free steps. In this way, Resistance is fooled into believing that every change is an insignificant one and never realises how enormous your transformation over time becomes. Small steps will allow you to adjust the experiments to your experiences and newly learned skills, in much the same way the terrain defines where you put your foot next.

[**]   Please note that not confirming your hypothesis is NOT a failure. You have learned something from your experiment. A failure is not having a hypothesis to start with or abandoning your experiment altogether.

[***]   Plus, you are leading human beings whose behaviour has millennia-long record of escaping reason and logic.

Think of experiments as little bets that decrease the uncertainty of what your leadership practice should be.* You can see it as a game of poker where you observe the context as well as the other players and, based on their behaviour, you decide how you want to play your cards. Having a hypothesis and success and failure criteria for your experiment will help you not to abandon it or to alter your approach before you see the result. It will make you stick with what you are trying out. This is what the weekly experiments are there for — whether you wish to bet on the biggest bang for your buck or reach for the lowest hanging fruit whatever you change will impact your leadership practice and make you understand it better.**

---

*   You can never have a complete set of information to assess the outcome. Plenty of information will stay hidden from you. Therefore, it is ok to say that you are not sure what the result is and you may want to repeat that experiment again to gather more data. But see it as a new separate experiment rather than a continuation of the previous one. In that way you will have a moment to look back and see what you've learned. Adjust your hypothesis and your success criteria, and, of course, set a new deadline. See it as a constant yet agile way to improve, where you stay tuned to the changes in yourself and in your environment, so that you are able to devise your optimal leadership practice.

**   Whatever experiments you might consider, write them up in your reflection journal and then leave them for the future. I am sure once this experimentation habit gets into your bloodstream, you won't let them go untested for long after you complete this course.

As you are embarking on the adventure deep within yourself, your first task will be to look around you for leaders you admire as well as those you are not a big fan of. What aspects of their attitude and behaviour resonate with you? What do you find unacceptable? Once you create an initial definition of what good leadership means to you, try to capture how you are being perceived by others. Understanding the essence of who you are as a leader creates a departure point for your transformation.

Define your first experiment. Think of something small, like starting a meeting differently, or answering emails only in the afternoon. Hypothesise what would be a result of this experiment. Perhaps your team open up more when you start a meeting with humour. Maybe you will progress with working on strategy when you don't have to attend to emails every minute. Try it out for at least three days and then evaluate. What changed? Did it help? If yes, how could you improve on it further? If not, what can you learn from that?

YOUR FIRST EXPERIMENT FOR THIS WEEK IS:
Describe it in three sentences

Your deadline   ....

Positive observations   Negative observations

✓ ✗

Positive reactions   ☺   ☹   Negative reactions

Your conclusion ....

What to improve further? ....

CORE TASKS

1. Look around. Who do you consider to be a good and a bad leader? (You can think about people at work but also those in your personal life or even historical figures).* List a few good and bad leaders and write down the qualities that make them good or bad in your eyes. Consider how each of the good leaders could further tweak their practice to be even better. Then think what would be the first step for the bad leaders to improve. Look back at what you wrote and think of how you would define a good and a bad leader.

    The qualities of a good leader are:
    - ....
    - ....
    - ....

    They could further improve by:
    - ....
    - ....
    - ....

    Good leaders are leaders who:
    - ....
    - ....
    - ....

    The qualities of a bad leader are:
    - ....
    - ....
    - ....

    They could start improving by:
    - ....
    - ....
    - ....

    Bad leaders are leaders who:
    - ....
    - ....
    - ....

*   If you can't find any good examples, jump to the next task.

2. Reflect on what leadership means to you. How do you define leadership practice?

    A good leader should be like / should do / should focus on ....

    ....

    An ideal leader **for me** should be like / should do / should focus on ....

    ....

    To me, leaderships mean ....

    ....

3. Knowing what you know now, think of what kind of leader you would like to be.

    As a great leader, I want to be ....

    Things I dream of being able to do as a leader are ....

4. Try to find out what others think of your leadership style. You can talk to your peers, subordinates and superiors, send a survey or consciously observe how others react to you as a leader. Write down your insights. Be mindful to focus on the positive as much as the negative feedback. What does it tell you about yourself?

    The positive feedback tells me ....

    The negative feedback tells me ....

5. It's time for some devil's advocate statements. Think about what would happen if you decided to change your leadership practice. What would those who represent your Resistance say? See that Resistance for what it is — a way to keep you conforming to the status quo, to keep you unchanged.

    ☐ You are not the leader we thought you were.
    ☐ You are getting soft.
    ☐ You are not as effective as you were before.
    ☐ You are losing your edge.
    ☐ You are...
    ☐ ...
    ☐ ...
    ☐ ...

EXTRAS

1. Reflect on your work and yourself as a leader. Do this in the form of long-writing stream of consciousness, motivated by three questions:

    • What do I think?

    • What do I feel?

    • Why do I think and feel this way?

    This is the beginning of your reflective practice, the practice that will get you to places you don't expect to find yourself in. Such practice will most likely calm you down and help you gain distance from the things that are happening.

2. Think back to how you defined leadership and leadership style. What do you envy when you look at great leaders? List ten qualities of good leaders that you think are missing or are underdeveloped in you.

    ....
    ....
    ....
    ....
    ....

    How can you become more like them?

    ....
    ....
    ....
    ....

3. Go for a walk and give yourself the time to think about your leadership.

LOOKING BACK

The first week is behind you. It means that the adventure has already begun. It is hard to see where it will take you but it is what adventures are about, isn't it? Remember to check in with yourself every week. Focus on the things that capture your attention as these are the aspects that are important to you.

Now, look more specifically back at the previous week:

1. How many tasks did you manage to complete? How did they help you? Where were you stuck?

2. Did you run your experiment this week? What was it? What was the outcome? Was it noticed by others around you? Is it something you plan to continue with? Or perhaps you have another idea of how to alter and improve on it?

3. Was there anything else that stuck with you? What was it? Why do you think it was important? How does it help you define your unique leadership practice?

Understanding Your Inner Voice

Beliefs

Irrational beliefs

Emotional labour

This week's challenge

Your core job as a leader is to be a catalyst whenever
the situation calls for change and then create the conditions
for that change to happen. To achieve this, you need to face
the voice in your head that dictates your perspective —
your rational and irrational beliefs, and also the self-
sabotaging mechanisms that might obstruct you from
getting where you want to go. Only then you can let go
of what doesn't serve you well and to be guided by
a clear picture of what is going on around you,
what you can influence and what is beyond your reach.

G areth, the vice-president of a girls-only boarding school in Canada, faced the following dilemma. He had just completed the process of choosing the next student council representative. This was an important role at his school since the chosen representative was allowed to sit in on every school meeting and had a vote on decisions about a variety of strategic topics pertinent to student life and learning conditions. Fourteen candidates entered the process, which was conducted much like a political campaign. At the end of that process there was one winner, leaving thirteen girls who weren't chosen. Gareth was preparing for a meeting with those girls during which he was supposed to let them know that they had not won. He planned to 'drop the bomb' — tell them they had not been selected, and then let the news sink in silence. He admitted that this was the way he would prefer to have such news delivered. Gareth's inner voice was telling him that once you hear disappointing news, you need a moment to mentally regroup while showing a brave face towards others to demonstrate that you are all right with the outcome, and that it's not much of a problem that you weren't chosen.

When I heard Gareth's plan, I imagined myself facing such news. What would be my first thought? It would be that I wasn't good enough to be chosen. This is the inner voice of many women, a product of decades, if not centuries, of how a female role was defined in society. If Gareth's goal was to put these girls down and make them feel bad, the 'bomb' approach was the way to go. But, of course, his goal was the opposite. He wanted to praise them for daring to run in the elections and to make them feel confident that although they didn't win, they were amazing, brave, young women, and to encourage them to continue pursuing their goals and dreams. Yet, he planned to act in a way that, although was probably natural for him, would have achieved the opposite effect from the one he wanted for the girls. Only after hearing his inner voice and imagining theirs, was he able to change his course of action and plan a different (and much more successful) meeting from the one he initially envisioned.

Our inner voice is a powerful force that dictates our notion of the self. It takes the form of a constant narrative going on in our heads. This narrative is used by the brain as a constructive tool to facilitate cognitive and emotional processing, and is influenced by both our conscious and subconscious views of and assumptions about the world. The story in our minds determines to a large extent how we see and interpret what's going on around us. Imagine this voice as a sports commentator. They never shut up, do they? * As much as you experience your inner voice, every person around you also experiences such a voice in their heads. It is as vivid and as conflicted as that in yours. It makes them think they are in the right and others are in the wrong. The same likely happens to you. Your inner voice defines your reality. And what defines inner voice? Your beliefs.

Beliefs

When I was a teenager, I wrote a story about a boy struggling in a family of alcoholics. My mother found that story and demanded that I never show it to anyone because it was exposing "the dirt of somebody else's life". This situation created a belief in me that I shouldn't show my sensitivity to others and, most certainly, I shouldn't expose others' vulnerability to the world. The older I became, the more this belief shaped

---

*   It is not just a voice that we hear. Russell Hurlburt, a psychologist from the University of Nevada, further noted inner seeing (of images of things you've seen in real life or imaginary visuals); inner emotions, such as anger or happiness; sensory awareness (like being aware of the grass when you walk barefoot); and unsymbolised thinking, a thought that doesn't manifest as words or images, but is undoubtedly present in your mind. Additionally, you can experience inner taste, like getting a bitter or sweet taste in your mouth when you hear someone talking about a certain food, or even become thirsty just by hearing a story of someone traveling through a desert. There is inner smell (like remembering a smell of a lake or sea)—perhaps less noticed as real smells usually are rather strong—or inner sensory perception, when you can imagine how the fur of a cat feels.[11]

my personal narrative and therefore my behaviour. I concluded that sharing emotions was a bad thing and that I needed to stay calm and reserved at all cost. Obviously, this was a pile of nonsense. Every one of us is exposed to the emotions of others and therefore, much like psychotherapists do, needs to have a space to express their emotions too. In my particular case, this habit led me to hold my breath, which signalled to my brain that I was in a constant state of panic. As you may imagine, all of this led me to start experiencing panic attacks that stopped me from making decisions and eventually caused burnout. And though I am now actively working on my ability to express emotions and to be vulnerable, this belief is impacting me even now as I write, taking the form of an inner voice, telling me that I shouldn't be sharing any of this with you.*

Beliefs like the one I mentioned deeply affect how we react to the world. They are the lens through which we see everything that happens. The American psychologist Albert Ellis classified such beliefs as either rational or irrational.[12] The former include beliefs supported by logical reasoning, as well as empirical and pragmatic data. Typically, they are flexible and non-extreme, and we have a deducible way to validate or falsify them. Rational beliefs usually provoke valid emotional responses that help us achieve our goals. Irrational beliefs, on the other hand, are scripts we have in our heads about how we believe life 'should' be for us and others (much like my attitude towards expressing my sensitivity).[13] These scripts are based on unfounded attitudes, opinions, and perspectives we hold that are out of synchrony with the way the world really is. They often cause us to experience negative responses to stressful situations (hence my panic attacks) and suboptimal, often stereotypical, ways of solving problems that are caused by life's pressures.

---

*   For leaders who have to deal with their own emotions and the emotions of others, the need for a safe space to 'discharge' is even more important. The less time it takes you for your own discharge, the more time you are able to spend on the objective and the team.

Irrational beliefs

Like I mentioned, our irrational beliefs are usually based on the ideas, feelings, ways of thinking, attitudes, opinions, biases, prejudices, and values with which we were raised. They might even have been true in the time frame in which you picked them up but as you grew up and as society has evolved, they have lost their truthfulness.* Yet, we have become accustomed to applying these beliefs of ours when faced with problems in our current life, even when they are not productive in helping us find constructive solutions. On the surface, they may even look appropriate for the occasion, but actually, they stimulate 'the least effort', habitual or counterproductive ways of thinking, giving us comfort and security in the short term, yet not resolving, but rather exacerbating, problems in the long run. For some of us, these ways of thinking can take the shape of negative, cynical, dogmatic, fatalistic or pessimistic ways of looking at life.** In others, irrational beliefs can manifest as overly optimistic or idealistic ways of seeing the world and the events that take place in it.

Whatever these irrational beliefs are, they are ways of thinking about ourselves that are out of context with facts.*** Irrational beliefs make us confused about the intentions of others as we project our assumptions onto them without verifying their correctness for either a person or a situation. They lead us to express negative or inefficient behaviours, such as anger, impulsivity, and inflexibility.[14] What makes it really scary is this: if irrational beliefs dominate, rational beliefs won't be able to overcome the effects of irrational thinking or, in the best case scenario have a 'minority vote' most likely making it impossible for you to get a good perspective on what's going on.[15] So, to control your inner voice,

---

*   In almost every civilisation, we see young generations push the borders of established beliefs, which is a way to question the 'old truths' that may not have the justification anymore.

**   Such ways include accepting loss without fight, seeking conflict, unnecessary risk-taking and rejection of positive (or even any) change.

***   They may result in our either under-valuing or over-valuing ourselves.

you need to understand the beliefs that control you (both irrational and rational).[16] It starts by understanding your personal and cultural story.*

Once you can capture your beliefs, you will be able to see which of them are serving you and which are jeopardising your actions as a leader. For example, anger is a great indicator that your beliefs are clashing with the world.** Whenever you experience anger (or frustration), very likely there is an underlying belief there. Such anger can be (and too often is) fuel for action but I would suggest that it should become fuel for reflection. Once you experience it, you have a chance to catch the underlying belief and see in what way it affects your thinking and actions. If you consider it a rational belief, it means that it should be cultivated. If it is irrational, something should be done about it, shouldn't it? In a way, your mind is like a garden of beliefs; if you decimate or remove the weeds (the irrational beliefs) the plants you want to live by (the rational beliefs) can grow and strengthen.

Next to noting your anger, you can capture your irrational beliefs by detecting situations in which you find yourself caught in a vicious circle, when whatever you do to resolve a problem seems to generate a bigger one. Another way to spot such beliefs is to pay attention to problems that you've been facing for a long time (you might even obsess about them) but you haven't taken a single step to address them.***

One more signal that you are acting on an irrational belief is when you choose a course of action only to find out that you are unhappy with it, and yet still you keep on pursuing it rather than looking for alternatives. Every leader will eventually face situations run by their irrational beliefs and it is crucial to understand how they affect your way of thinking and

---

*   I, for example, am defined by the Catholic tradition in which I was raised and although I don't see myself as a religious person, I know that many of my values and ways of seeing the world are deeply rooted in the Christian religion and how that was expressed around me when I was a child.

**   In *The Artist's Way* Julia Cameron writes that "anger is a map".

***   For example, you might be afraid to pursue a certain course of action because of the guilt you feel or you might find yourself immobilised to even face that problem, so you avoid it, deny it, procrastinate about it, ignore it, run away from it or turn your back on it.

acting. If you don't solve your irrational beliefs, your team might copy them (much like children do), resulting in an unwanted amplification of the problems you want to avoid in the first place.

Emotional labour

As much as it is crucial to capture and understand your beliefs, it is not enough.[17] Consider that "our emotions and behaviours are not directly determined by life events, but rather by the way these events are cognitively processed and evaluated".[18] You yourself have the ability to alter the narrative you tell yourself through the actions that reinforce the beliefs you want to strengthen and abandon those you find are no longer serving you. It will help you to become a productive, realistic problem solver. Your fear (or guilt) will shrink and it you will be able to put the problems you face into a realistic perspective as to their importance, magnitude, and the probability of being solved. You will find yourself being more honest with yourself and able to separate your feelings from the content of the problem. This, in turn, will enable you to have a healthier perspective with a greater sense of direction, to recognise your self-worth, and separate it from the errors and mistakes you have made and will make in the future.

There is one thing that is required through — emotional labour.* Seth Godin calls emotional labour, "the work of doing what we don't necessarily feel like doing, the work of being a professional, the work of engaging with others in a way that leads to the best long-term outcome."[19] Emotional labour requires guts. You have to be brave to challenge your assumptions.

---

*   Imagine you are a four-year old version of yourself locked away in a laboratory. In front of you, there is a delicious looking cupcake. But before you are allowed to reach out and dive into it, the boring looking adult offers you a choice: you can have this one cupcake now or you can have two of them a little later. Which would you choose? I am not sure what my four-year old self would have done, to be perfectly honest. I would like to imagine that I would have waited, but would I? This process of waiting is an example of emotional labour.

Resistance will tell you not to do so, as it can be quite confronting to realise that you have believed or acted in a 'wrong' way for so long.[*] Emotional labour also requires brutal honesty about what you are good and bad at so that you can build on your strengths and compensate for your weaknesses.

You can practice emotional labour on two levels: shallow or deep.[20] Shallow labour means that you express certain behaviour on the surface but you do not alter how you see the world or feel about it. Your inner voice is still the same, your irrational beliefs continue holding a firm position but on the surface, you do your best to appear as if something changed. But here's a challenge. If you choose to do shallow labour, not only do you run the risk of someone calling your bluff but what's more, it can be harmful to your mental and physical health.[21] On the other hand, if you choose to turn your emotional labour into an effortful process through which you change your beliefs, your feelings, and your actions, you will not only be perceived as an authentic leader but it will also improve your life overall.[**, 22]

---

[*]   The way to deal with this 'sorrow' is not to label it as a 'wrong' way but just as your 'old' way.

[**]   The fact is that you've already started doing so. You just need to keep on going with patience and perseverance.

WEEK

11

CHALLENGE

Your task this week will include dissecting your beliefs to see which of the narratives you are running in your head are built on rational beliefs, and which on irrational ones. Reflect on your emotions and consider what triggers them. Think back to your childhood to see what your origin story is. You may even dig deeper to see what stories were run by your family, your teachers, your friends. How many of these are no longer relevant?

YOUR EXPERIMENT FOR THIS WEEK IS:
Describe it in three sentences

Your deadline ....

Positive observations   Negative observations

√ ✗

Positive reactions   ☺ ☹   Negative reactions

Your conclusion ....

What to improve further? ....

CORE TASKS

1. Do some detective work to find out what angers you. You could include others in this task too, if they were involved when you got angry recently. Investigate the context in which it happened. List five beliefs that seem to underline your reaction.

   1. ....
   2. ....
   3. ....
   4. ....
   5. ....

2. Take one issue that angers you the most as a leader (you can select one from the list from above or think of something new). Answer the following questions.[23]

   - Am I the owner of the problem or am I angry because the owner of the problem isn't solving it? YES / NO

   - Am I going round in circles trying to solve this problem? YES / NO

   - Is there something in me that keeps me from taking the necessary action? YES / NO

   - Am I bothered by the thoughts of what I or others 'should do, act like, think, or feel'? YES / NO

   - Do I keep on saying how this situation 'should be,' rather than facing how it really is? YES / NO

   - Am I hoping that by some miracle it will resolve itself? YES / NO

   - Am I burdened by the fear of what others will think of me in this situation? YES / NO

   - Do I know what the solution is, but I am paralysed to act? YES / NO

   - Do I find myself using a lot of 'yes but's' in discussing this problem? YES / NO

- Am I procrastinating, avoiding, ignoring, or running away from this problem? YES / NO

- Is this problem causing much distress for me and others, and yet I can't resolve it? YES / NO

If you found yourself answering: YES to some (or most) of these questions, you are likely to have just bumped up against one or more of your irrational beliefs.

3. Try to get to the bottom of that belief. First, consider, what stops you from acting. List at least five reasons why you are not resolving this problem. Consider:

   - Is what stops me from acting something I have believed in all my life?

   - Is the thing that stops me coming from my parents, church, family, peers, work, society, culture, community, race, ethnic reference group, or social network?

   - Is it something that recurs when I try to solve problems similar to this one?

   - Do I feel dishonest with myself when thinking about this problem?

   - Am I feeling guilty or fearful of rejection as I face this problem?

   Can you state the belief that affects your action? If yes, write it down:
   My belief is ....
   ....
   ....

4. You have now captured your belief. You could ask yourself the question Byron Katie asks, "Could the opposite of your belief be true too?"[24] You can also unpack it through the following questions:

   - Is there any basis, in reality, to support this belief as always being true? YES / NO

   - Does it encourage personal growth, emotional maturity, independent thinking and action, and stable mental health? YES / NO

- Will this belief help you overcome this and future problems of this kind? YES / NO

- Will acting upon this belief be self-defeating for you? YES / NO

- Does it protect you and your rights as a person? YES / NO

- Does it assist you in connecting honestly and openly with others? YES / NO

- Does it help you be a creative, rational problem solver who can identify a series of alternatives from which you can choose the best one? YES / NO

- Does it stifle your thinking to the point of immobilisation? YES / NO

- When you tell others about this belief do they support you because that is the way everyone in your family, peer group, work, church, or community thinks? YES / NO

- Is this belief absolute? Is it a black or white, yes or no, win or lose, no options in the middle type of belief? YES / NO

Answers pointing at a rational belief are: 1 - NO, 2 - YES, 3 - YES, 4 - NO, 5 - YES, 6 - YES, 7 - YES, 8 - NO, 9 - NO, 10 - NO.

If you gave different answers to one or more questions, then your blocking belief is most likely irrational. If you were to phrase that belief once again, how would you do it?

My irrational belief is ....

and it is caused by ....

or (if you found a rational one)

My rational belief is ....

and it is built upon ....

You can further ask yourself whether this cause planted more irrational beliefs in your mind. If yes, what are they?

5. Let's alter this belief. Consider the following questions:

   - What would be a better belief to substitute for this irrational belief?

   - How would I feel if I substituted this new belief for my irrational belief?

   - How will I grow if I decide to follow this new belief?

   - How will I let others grow if I decide to follow this new belief?

   - What is keeping me from accepting this new belief?

   Now, it is time to explicate your new rational belief.

   My new rational belief is ....

   and it will help me ....

   If you think you didn't quite land on a rational belief here, you can repeat this exercise and see what changes. You can further use it to face other beliefs you hold and see whether they are based on rational thinking or maybe they should also be altered.

6. It is time to start the unbelieving process about how you see leadership. Think back to Week 1. How did you define leadership? Answer these questions for yourself. Be brutally honest.

   - Is what I believe about leadership rational or irrational? What are the rational beliefs that I hold? What are the irrational ones? If I were to revisit my definition of leadership, how would I alter it?

   - Why do I want to be a leader? What makes me want to lead? What part of this desire comes from the expectations of me by my parents, my culture, etc.? What is my genuine need? What of this belief is verifiable and what is a belief that was installed in me by 'the system'?

   - What are the systems that define my beliefs about leadership? Which of them are healthy and nurturing and which are holding me to habits I'd rather not express anymore?

   - If I had all the freedom to define it — how would I like to lead?

EXTRAS

1. Try to capture your inner voice. Are the stories you tell yourself rather positive or negative? Choose one story and see how it affects the way you see the situation or person it refers to. What could be an alternative explanation of what happened? What would be the most positive explanation? How does thinking about the different explanations change your outlook?

2. Think back to growing up (your family, your school, your sports team, your choir, you name it). What were the values you were raised in? What were you punished for? What is your culture story? How does it affect the way you see yourself today?

3. Do something for yourself, something that you think doesn't quite suit you (like swinging on a swing, building a sand castle or getting a massage). See how it feels to do it anyway. What kind of belief was hiding behind you thinking that it is not for you?

LOOKING BACK

Look back at the past week and start by praising yourself. The emotional labour you are putting in is already working its magic even if you may not see it just yet. Notice what naturally draws your attention and what scares you. All these aspects are helping you become the leader you want to be.

Now, look more specifically back at the previous week:

1. How many core tasks did you manage to complete? How did they help you? Where were you stuck?

2. Did you run your experiment this week? What was it? What was the outcome? Was it noticed by others around you? Is it something you plan to continue with? Or perhaps you have another idea of how to alter and improve on it?

3. Was there anything else that stuck with you? What was it? Why do you think it was important? How does it help you define your unique leadership practice?

The Best Version of You

Finding your purpose

Imposter syndrome

The meaning of good enough

Mindset of generosity

The art of possibility

This week's challenge

Everyone carries within them the best possible version
of themselves. Deep down, you know what kind of leader
you have the potential to be. This potential is driven by
your purpose, the driving force rooted in your personal
narrative that makes you get out of bed every day and
keep on carrying on. But there is also a force that works
against you, imposter syndrome, making you feel that
you are not good enough to become who you have
the potential to be. Is there a way to overcome it?

I have good and bad news to start with. The bad news is that we see only about 5% of what's happening around us. This characteristic of our brain was noted by the father of psychology, William James, who wrote:

> "Millions of items of the outward order are present to my senses which never properly enter into my experience. Why? Because they have no interest for me. My experience is what I agree to attend to. Only those items which I notice shape my mind".[25]

What he observed (confirmed by today's neuroscience) is that from the billions of stimuli we are exposed to, we orient only towards those that we believe are worth noticing. We choose what to focus on based on whether it is urgent, dangerous, or perhaps appealing, but above all, based on how well it fits the narrative we tell ourselves about our lives.[26] Have you heard of 'the invisible gorilla' experiment? [27, 28, 29] It beautifully demonstrates this very quality of our brain.

Spoiler alert: I'm going to describe what happens in that movie,
so you might want to watch it before reading any further.

In this experiment, you are invited to watch a video in which two groups of basketball players (one dressed in black and the other in white) are passing a ball. You are directed to count the number of passes among the white team. Easy enough. Yet, after the experiment is over and you triumphantly announce the result of your counting, the experimenter asks you whether you saw a gorilla. What gorilla?

Once your attention is repurposed and you watch that same video again, you will see a person in a gorilla costume passing through the scene, stopping in the middle of the group of players and pounding their chest. How was it possible to miss it? Yet, you did. And I did.

Thousands of other people did too. The eye-gazing data shows that while doing this experiment, participants are looking directly at the gorilla and yet still do not see it. The reason for this is simple. Your attention was focused on the white team and their actions, so your brain ignored the black team, including the gorilla who was dressed in black as well. That doesn't sound good, does it? But there is a piece of good news too. It is the fact that we can choose what that 5% we notice is. This is why it is crucial to understand what drives you as a person and as a leader, to understand your purpose.

Finding your purpose

Living a purposeful life is, according to Victor Frankl, "the primary motivational force" in people.[30] Martin Seligman defines it as, "belonging to and serving something that you believe is bigger than the self".[31] On a personal level, it is your guide to choosing how to live your life and what to strive for. It guides your personal goals and it helps you make sense of what happens to you. For example, as I am sitting here writing these words, I can see how it reflects my purpose, and therefore, I am willingly giving up all the other things I could be doing instead. In the context of your work, your purpose helps you align your values with your actions and with your definition of success.[32]

Much like beliefs, purpose is rooted in your personal story and aligned to the image of who you are in your own eyes. It is an animating force that mobilises you — it helps you make decisions, provokes action, and drives ethical behaviour. Purpose makes you want to get out of bed and lead with energy, enthusiasm, and conviction even if the day ahead doesn't promise only perks. Finally, having purpose positively impacts your physical and mental health much more than simply feeling happy.[33]

Imposter syndrome

Discovering your purpose is necessary but not sufficient to keep the fire inside you burning. As I mentioned before, Resistance is working against you and will do whatever is in its power to derail you. It might make you feel like you don't belong. It may convince you that you are not good leadership material, that you don't quite deserve this role you have been given, and that the accomplishments you are authoring are not really yours. As a result, you might become afraid that you are going to be found out by your team, or by someone else in your organisation, as a fraud. It is something about 70% of all people experience at some point in their lives and it is called imposter syndrome.[34]

There is no data I have been able to find that shows how frequently it happens to leaders but from my empirical observations, imposter syndrome occurs often, probably even too often, especially early on in their leadership careers. Let's be honest, whenever we embark on something new, we are not very good at it. It doesn't matter if you are a junior clerk or a CEO, you need to grow into that role and that takes time. I am flabbergasted that nobody tells us this, so we continue feeling like an imposter. We all should be told that 'of course you are not a 100% match, but we strongly believe that you can grow towards that 100%'. This would make it so much easier to accept our own imperfection, wouldn't it?

As we are often thrown into the deep waters of leadership without much support, we end up allowing the critic in our heads to grab the steering wheel of our internal dialogue. The critic uses its best logic 'against' us. It leads us to either over-prepare or to procrastinate as a way of avoiding 'being caught out' as incompetent. As soon as we fall prey to imposter syndrome, whatever success we achieve, we are likely to discredit it as not related to our skill and competence but as luck.[35] We fall prey to self-doubt, holding far too high standards for ourselves, leading to over-generalisation of failures, stress, and maladaptive behaviour that is caused by our need to be 'the best', whatever 'the best' means.[*, 36] Instead, it would be a much better if we just openly communicated that we are growing into our role, every day a step and sometimes a skip and jump.

* Actually, there seem to be five so-called *competence types*[37] which represent the different mindsets you might fall into when you experience imposter syndrome—the Perfectionist, the Superwoman / man, the Natural Genius, the Soloist and the Expert. The Perfectionist sets excessively high goals for themselves, and when they fail to reach them, they experience major self-doubt and worry about measuring up. The Superwoman / man pushes themselves to work harder and harder to measure up and too often becomes a workaholic addicted to the validation that comes from working, not to the work itself. The Natural Genius judges their competence based how easy it is to master it so if they take a long time to master something, they feel ashamed and fraudulent. The Soloist assumes everything needs to be done by them and refuses any help, worrying that asking for help reveals their phoniness. Finally, the Expert measures their competence based on 'what' and 'how much' they know or can do. Believing they will never know enough, they fear being exposed as inexperienced or unknowledgeable.

Where does imposter syndrome come from? As you might have guessed, it stems from our home environment, family dynamics, and parenting styles, also from school and education, but most of all from various stereotypes related to race, gender or where you were raised.[38] For example, your imposter syndrome may be caused by you having been told that your skills are atypical in comparison with other members of your family, being convinced that success requires little effort and is based on intellectual capability, or by having rarely experienced positive reinforcement.[*, 39] Another trigger for imposter syndrome might come from always being compared to others and judged as worse or as better. When you were told you are not measuring up to your colleagues at school, you might have a hard time to believe that you are good enough. On the other hand, if you were told that you are better than others (or even the best), you might feel like whatever you do in life doesn't match these early achievements of your, so you are not performing as expected. You can also experience it if you were told that certain things are expected from you as a man or a woman that mismatch with your natural talents and capabilities.

Regardless of what caused it, imposter syndrome feeds off the feeling so many of us experience: of not being good enough. It eats up any happiness coming from our successes. It will make you live in constant fear, which will eventually lead to emotional exhaustion, loss of internal motivation, decrease in your achievements, feeling of dissatisfaction, shame, anxiety, and eventually, burnout.[41] It won't allow you to enjoy yourself as a leader. Do we have to succumb to it though?

The meaning of good enough

As I mentioned earlier, we only see about 5% of what's happening around us. This is because, although we have a great sensory bandwidth, we have an even better filtering mechanism that selects

---

*   As a consequence, imposter syndrome may take a form of perfectionism expressed by setting for yourself a self-fulfilling prophecy of "excessively high, unrealistic goals and then experience self-defeating thoughts and behaviours when they can't reach those goals".[40] Perfectionism is another belief we hold on to that needs to be dismantled as it is one that belongs in the realm of irrationality. If you hold on to it, it will lead you to hide your mistakes and stubbornly stick to your opinions even if you already know you are not quite right.

what becomes conscious to us. The things we notice determine our reality and our identity. What we don't quite realise is that our identities are often a compensation for when we were made aware we were not good enough, therefore, most likely not loveable.[42] We, therefore, created strategies to prove to ourselves that this is not true. We wanted to believe we were smart and funny and... [insert your own hopes here]. We tried to be good at that something to get some sort of validation of our *enoughness*. The next step was easy. We identified with that image of ours, only to find ourselves in radical competition with anyone else with a similar metric. So, we found ourselves competing with our peers, our enemies, even members of our team. This competitiveness is often called ambition, less often ego.*

Yet, your enoughness is not limited to wealth, position, status, or any such simplistic ways of judging yourself. They are just a few tiny aspects of who you are. If you allow yourself to see yourself as a multidimensional and unique human being, you won't reduce yourself to the one part of that picture anymore. You will also realise that everyone else is unique too. This is a way to help yourself start to understand your unique self, with your particular skills and contribution, which is fundamentally in no competition with anyone else. As much as you have something to offer, so does every other person.

Of course, battling those early preconceptions of your not-enoughness is tough work. Fortunately, neuroplasticity helps you deal with it, as it gives you the means to refocus what you see. Imagine that you find your status threatened at work. Someone told you, for example, that you didn't do whatever you were supposed to do as well as they thought you should have. Such a situation will almost for sure trigger the feeling of not-enoughness, causing you to either defend yourself, withdraw or counterattack. You are likely to have such a reaction

---

* I have a friend who realised she identified herself through her status. Her goal was to be seen as a Vice President or at least a director. At the same time, she found herself feeling utterly miserable when she was faced with company politics, where she had to compete with everyone else running the same status metrics. There is a problem with such metrics though: if anyone else is better at it than you, you start feeling not that valuable, your imposter syndrome kicks in and you are likely to act out in ways that are not optimal and certainly not healthy for you (and for others).

because you know that you did everything with your best intentions and commitment. This is why the comment you just heard makes you think less of yourself and you try to compensate for it. You put even more effort to achieve the expected outcome (much as in the saying, 'if brute force ain't solving the problem you are not using enough of it'). Once again you receive negative feedback. You are most likely feeling crushed. Yet, if you think about it, this action and this judgment don't define who you are. They don't even guarantee that whoever criticised you knows how what you did could have been done better. Often there is just no optimal way to do something, and 'there are many roads leading to Rome', yours likely being one of them.

Thus instead of falling into the vicious circle of succumbing to imposter syndrome, you could stop for a moment and hear this very comment again from a place of being good enough. How would it make you feel? Most likely you would realise that whatever it was about (even if there was some truth in the fact that you could have done things better), it represented only a tiny fragment of who you are and only for a small moment in time. It is a learning moment, not a general critique of you as a human being. Your perception is likely to shift once you see that you are far more than your actions, you will be able to become less judgmental towards what happened and towards yourself. It then allows you to change your position in the communication process with your 'judge' from the content level to the process level or even to the objective level. In that way you would train your brain to modify its structure and function in response to a similar experience in the future, so that you don't default to feeling not good enough. It becomes easier if you see the other person as a wholesome being much like yourself. This is what mindset of generosity helps with.

Mindset of generosity

The Ascent (a division of Motley Fool, an investment guidance organisation) conducted an intriguing survey of 1010 people in the U.S., which showed that 81% of those who reported being more generous felt a greater sense of purpose in their lives, compared to 60% of those who reported being less generous.[43] What's more, this sense of generosity made respondents feel more successful in their careers and happier within their organisations (and probably in their private lives as well).

Generosity is proven to make us feel closer to others, more satisfied with the people around us, and happier with our bosses.* In many ways, generosity can breathe new life into your purpose and increase your sense of self-worth. How does it manifest?

Firstly, it is crucial to point out that generosity is explicated in the deep connection with ourselves and with people around us. You can't be generous with others if your sense of self-worth, your enoughness, is not solid in you. Once you find in yourself the space for self-generosity you will be able to extend it to others. If you feel worthy, you won't have as much trouble making others feel worthy too.**

The more self-generous you feel, the more you are open to learning about yourself, and consequently, you are much more open to seeing others as learners too, which offers them an increased level of self-confidence (as a sort of a positive feedback loop). Thus, generosity is about taking time to share the finite resources that are most scarce for any leader, such as time, attention, kindness, and care. It is about creating a safety net — the conditions for trust, vulnerability, and learning (this is something we will return to later). But generosity is as much about giving as it is about accepting help from others. Many leaders tend to assume that they need to have all the answers, that not knowing is a sign of weakness, of letting their teams down. As you might have guessed, this stems from the lack of self-generosity which is triggered by an irrational belief that leadership is about knowing answers, when in fact it is about creating the conditions so that others have the space to find the answers themselves. The big question is how to do it.

The art of possibility

When we see the world from the perspective of not being good enough, we tend to judge everything in terms of success or failure. I was asked for an opinion — success. I wasn't invited to the table — failure.

---

* 70% of those who reported being more generous said they were satisfied with their career compared to 49% of those who reported being less generous. 71% of those who reported being more generous said they were satisfied with their companies compared to 54% of those who reported being less generous.

** You will also find more time for other people as you do not feel the need to spend so much time on yourself.

It seems like everything is black-and-white. But there are practices out there that will help you see such situations in different shades of grey. I would like to highlight three of them.[44]

The first practice is about seeing yourself as *a contributor* rather than a leader. Imagine that you are in a meeting where a new project is being fiercely discussed. What often happens is that we try to impose our ideas on others assuming that we know what the optimal approach might be. We may not be a leader of this project but we certainly act like one (and so do others which too often causes arguments and unnecessary tension). The alternative is to choose to share your perspective but let others (preferably the project leaders) pick what they want to consider and not consider for now. In that way you switch your mindset to the one of *a contributor* — a person who offers the best possible advice but doesn't expect this advice to be treated as a demand. Such a perspective doesn't have a dark side, there is no negative feeling attached to it. If someone uses your suggestions, that's great, but if they don't it was their choice to do so, so it doesn't reflect on you in any way. It is a fantastic mindset to come to work with. Imagine how it would feel if after getting out of bed, you would consider for a moment: 'How can I contribute today?'

The second practice is about *giving yourself an A* before you start doing anything. There is scientific proof that we all are born with an amazing set of skills and talents.[45] Yet somehow we end up believing this is not the case (We've looked into some of the reasons for it already).* Thus, *giving yourself an A* is a practice of self-acceptance, which it turn helps you to deal with any obstacles you meet on your path. If you know you are going to succeed because you have already graded yourself, whatever failure happens to take place, it is just learning that helps you to get the best possible result.

Imagine that you are about to have a difficult conversation with your boss. For example, you want them to accept a new, possibly more risky plan of action with respect to the project you lead. I bet you are nervous and the predominant thought you experience is about them

*   It is easy to say that we need to abandon our irrational beliefs and create a feeling of self-worth but from personal experience, I know how hard it is and how much time is needed to progress on that path.

saying 'no' and you doing anything in your power to convince them otherwise. Instead, you can approach that conversation as if you already got their approval. The conversation will likely change in a way that you are not going to try to 'sell' your idea but rather discuss the best approach to take to make it happen. It is quite a shift, isn't it?

Or consider another scenario. You need to deliver some unpleasant news to your team, like, for example, that the bonuses are not going to be what they hoped for. If you *give yourself an A* you are likely to approach such a meeting as a discussion as to how else you can compensate them for the lack of financial award. Perhaps you can dedicate time to work on some good cause as a part of your skill development. Or maybe you could offer more work flexibility, so that they can be more present for their families. Whatever it is, if you approach such a conversation from a perspective of compassion and self-compassion, there will certainly be unexpected solutions presenting themselves. *Giving yourself an A* to yourself and others opens up a space for curiosity and alignment in getting the best possible outcome. It is a practice of trying out new approaches and alternative ways of thinking. It allows you to, paraphrasing the words of the Supreme Court Justice Thurgood Marshall, "do the best you can with what you have."

The third and final practice I would like to propose is called *Rule No 6*. Have you ever experienced a growing tension in your body, when you are in a meeting and suddenly feel that others are not listening to you or are not considering your opinion and insights? It physically feels like my muscles contract to form an armour. This tension is the most reliable sign of the feeling of not being attended to, of being one-down or, at worst, unnecessary. It gives existence to all your worst fears, which, in turn, entirely blocks any ounce of generosity. The story of *Rule No 6* is the best tool I know that gets you out of this mental state in which you start measuring yourself against others. It goes like this:

> "Two prime ministers are sitting in the room discussing affairs of state. Suddenly a man bursts in, apoplectic with fury, shouting and stamping and banging his fist on the desk. The resident prime minister admonishes him: 'Peter,' he says, 'kindly remember Rule No 6,' whereupon Peter is instantly restored to complete calm, apologises,

and withdraws. The politicians return to their conversation, only to be interrupted yet again twenty minutes later by a hysterical woman gesticulating wildly, her hair flying. Again, the intruder is greeted with the words: 'Marie, please remember Rule No 6.' Complete calm descends once more, and she too withdraws with a bow and an apology. When the scene is repeated for the third time, the visiting prime minister addresses his colleague: 'My dear friend, I've seen many things in my life, but never anything as remarkable as this. Would you be willing to share with me the secret of Rule No 6?' 'Very simple,' replies the resident prime minister. 'Rule No 6 is: Don't take yourself so g—damn seriously.' 'Ah,' says his visitor, 'that is a fine rule.' After a moment of pondering, he inquires, 'And what, may I ask, are the other rules?' 'There aren't any.'"[46]

Rule No 6 asks you to take yourself lightly — the best way to 'get over ourselves.' When I notice that I am taking myself too seriously (usually by realising that I am clenching my teeth or fists) I try to take a deep breath, think for a moment why I am so upset with the way things are and consider whether I am a leader or a contributor to what is happening (and usually it is the latter). Once I clarify that (only for myself), I *give myself an A* and apply some humour to relax the situation, even if the subject matter is dead-serious. Humour is the greatest weapon of *Rule No 6* as it brings us together, peels away the notion of entitlement, and sparks collaboration. Don't you love working with people who laugh and joke, and see the world from the perspective of lightness rather than heaviness? In humour, there is no space for arguing, jumping down each others' throats, or putting each other down. It clarifies miscommunications, calms tensions, and enables constructive feedback. It is the most collaborative mindset ever, full of possibilities not only to realise your purpose and potential but also to bring meaning to everybody involved.

WEEK

CHALLENGE

This week, we will dig into your your purpose. Purpose is the force that makes you face all obstacles with energy and stamina. We will also look at your strengths to start building a picture of your *enoughness*. If you find the time, we will try to unpack who sits on the committee that runs your head to figure out who you might want behind the steering wheel of your thinking (and perhaps the critic will, finally, have to move to the back seat).

YOUR EXPERIMENT FOR THIS WEEK IS:

Describe it in three sentences

Your deadline ....

Positive observations   Negative observations

✓   ✗

Positive reactions   ☺   ☹   Negative reactions

Your conclusion ....

What to improve further? ....

CORE TASKS

1. To identify your purpose, answer the following questions. You will get the same question multiple times, trust the process. Let it flow. Write answers to each question until you cannot answer that question anymore.

   1. What do I like to think about? Where does my mind wander?

   2. What do I care about? What matters to me?

   3. What is the contribution I want to make to the world or the lives of other people?

   4. What do I get out of doing what I do professionally? What does that mean to me?

   5. What else do I get out of it?

   6. Is there something else I get out of it?

   7. Why are those things important to me?

      a. Why is that important to me?

      b. Why is that important to me?

      c. And why is that so important to me?

   8. What kind of world will I find myself in by having those things?

   9. What kind of a world will that create for others?

   10. How would that make me fulfilled?

   11. Imagine that world: what does it look like?

   12. In what way is that world inspiring?

   13. How could it be inspiring to others?

   This vision of the world as you dream it is the basis for your purpose. If you were to phrase it in one sentence how might you do so?

   My purpose is to ....

   ....

   ....

2. Your strength comes from the things you love to do. Finish the following statements:

    I feel most alive when I ....

    ....is something I would do for (almost) nothing.

    When I do ....I lose track of time.

    I care most about ....

    It gives me the feeling of ultimate reward when I ....

    I am most passionate about ....

    I find it unbearable when ....

    The things I most like day in and day out are ....

    List ten of your strengths. Be as generous to yourself as you can. Give yourself an A if there is a skill you are in the process of developing. See yourself as being utterly good enough.

    ....

    ....

    ....

    ....

    ....

3. Imagine you are at the end of this course and the contributions you hope for are a reality. What would you praise yourself for? Write ten such praises.

    ....

    ....

    ....

    ....

    ....

4. Take yourself for a date. Go out just with yourself to a place you like. Think of three tiny changes you could make as a leader in order to take a step forward that builds on your purpose and/or strengths.

EXTRAS

1. There is an episode of the *The Big Bang Theory* where one of the main characters, Sheldon, falls asleep so his internal committee of personalities may assemble.[47] It's an apt representation of the fact that in our heads we are committees of the different selves. Think about what versions of you are the members of that committee and what are their roles. They are your protection mechanisms developed so that you were able to get where you are. Even though you might not want all of them to have a voice anymore, they all deserve your love and respect. They certainly helped you out once.

2. Most likely, one of the versions of you at the table is your inner critic, activating your imposter syndrome. Let's see what it feeds off:

    Why would you think you are not good enough? ....

    When do you procrastinate? ....

    In what ways you don't trust yourself? ....

    When do you feel like a fraud? ....

    Knowing this, let your inner critic speak. Think of ten aspects of yourself that don't allow you to become the leader you want to be:

    1. ....   6. ....
    2. ....   7. ....
    3. ....   8. ....
    4. ....   9. ....
    5. ....   10. ....

    Filter each of these points through the irrational beliefs exercise from last week. How many of them are something you just got yourself to believe? But even if some traits you unearthed are a true representation of you as a leader, it is important to realise that every quality we have has its bright and dark side. What is the bright side of your shortcomings?

LOOKING BACK

This is the third time you are doing your weekly check-in! You are well underway by now and, although it may not feel that way yet, the change is already happening. Look back over the past week. See what naturally draws your attention and what scares you. Whatever you see, you are doing great!

Now, look more specifically back at the previous week:

1. How many core tasks did you manage to complete? How did they help you? Where were you stuck?

2. Did you run your experiment this week? What was it? What was the outcome? Was it noticed by others around you? Is it something you plan to continue with? Or perhaps you have another idea of how to alter and improve on it?

3. If you were to give yourself an A for the next week, what would it be? Why?

4. Was there anything else that resonated with you? What was it? Why do you think it was important? How does it help you define your unique leadership practice?

Leading With Vision

We may choose to follow some people but much more likely we are keen to follow a vision they have. Vision is a magnet that brings us together, regardless of our varied purposes and personal stories. Vision ignites and motivates us to persist, even when things get hard. This is why it is so crucial to know what your vision is. The more clear your vision, the more effectively you can lead. Don't think that your vision needs to be innovative or groundbreaking (although it most certainly can). In fact it is as good if your vision fits with the goals of your organisation, is a part of a bigger whole.

Your purpose is not the same as your vision. Purpose defines you as an individual, it underlines why you are who you are. It is a part of your intrinsic reason for existence, defined by your past experiences, your growth path, your hopes and dreams. It is your deeply personal story. Everybody else has such a story too, a story that defines their purpose.

Most likely you will have one purpose in life. It may become more detailed as you mature and come to a greater understanding of yourself. But it is unlikely that your purpose will alter over your lifetime. If it does (because sometimes it happens) it is often caused by a radical change in your life, like becoming aware that you missed something or have just been plain wrong.*

Vision, on the other hand, is something that is designed to be shared. It is something that motivates you and others to pursue a common goal, something that is bigger than the sum of you all. Your vision can be different at a different organisation you are a part of. In a way, much like your purpose is set for you, the vision should be set for the organisation. In that way you can choose which organisational vision you want to contribute to. Think of it this way — your purpose is the roots but your vision is the tree.

Once again, context matters

As a leader, your role is to create and protect the conditions under which your vision can come to fruition. The reality is, however, that not all conditions are as you wish them to be. I once worked for an organisation that convinced me they were ready for transformation, only to waste nine months of my life before realising that they weren't.

---

*   I've seen people changing their purpose because they experienced something traumatic happening either to themselves or to their family and friends..

That painful lesson is best expressed by Dave Snowden, the founder of the Cognitive Edge Institute:

> "You can be the most brilliant leader in the history of humanity with the best ideas but if the context isn't right for a change it won't happen. If the conditions are right then the smallest push will set things moving. A lot of leadership is about constantly mapping that context, seeing where the *fitness* of the landscape is such that the energy cost of change could be less than the energy cost of staying as we are".[48]

Your context determines what is possible or impossible, easy or difficult. There are several aspects to it, such as market conditions, stakeholder expectations, overall organisational strategy and culture, that likely determine your actions. If you don't have a vision of where you want to go, you will be swayed by them.* The vision is a necessary baseline condition for progress to occur in the desired direction.** But it is as important to realise that your leadership practice needs to be aligned with the conditions you find yourself in. Some situations require transformative leaders who are able to lead change and engage people across the organisation. Some require leaders who keep the business running smoothly. There is nothing wrong with either. But this is definitely something to consider when you think about the impact you want to create.

The big question is whether the context you find yourself in is the context that helps you thrive and allows you to seek the change you hope for. If this is the situation, fantastic. But if that is not the case, you need to ask yourself: are you willing to stay and wait for the right moment, or would it be better to seek another organisation where you have the opportunity

---

* Whenever I think about it the following conversation between Alice and the Cheshire Cat rings in my ears,
"Would you tell me, please, which way I ought to go from here?"
"That depends a good deal on where you want to get to," said the Cat.
"I don't much care where—" said Alice.
"Then it doesn't matter which way you go," said the Cat. "
—so long as I get somewhere," Alice added as an explanation.
"Oh, you're sure to do that," said the Cat, "if you only walk long enough."

** And, sometimes, the environment you find yourself in is simply not ready for any of it. Even some leaders who had proved themselves in one of the most widely respected training grounds for leadership, GE, once they changed jobs, weren't as successful anymore. It wasn't them, it was the context.

to act at the pace and in the way you want? You can also choose a third option. You try to change your context bearing in mind that altering an organisational mindset is a difficult and lengthy endeavour.*

Don't beat yourself up if you decide to change organisations. It is not necessarily a reflection of you as a leader. Some places don't fit who you want to be. This is why many successful leaders change jobs after a few years. They have made the changes they wanted and are good at implementing. When they are asked to maintain the status quo, they often realise that it is not something they either excel at or want to do. So they move on. Changing jobs (or rather, changing context) is in fact a process of seeking a place to lead in a way that is aligned with you and your vision.

'Moonshot' or 'just cause'

Once you've positively assessed the potential your context offers you, the next step is to figure out what change you seek to make. Typically, a vision for such change is formulated in one of two ways — as a 'moonshot' (named after President Kennedy's vision for the US to be the first nation to get a man on the moon) or, as Simon Sinek describes it, a 'just cause'.[49] A moonshot has a finite time-frame with one winner at the finish line. An example of a moonshot would be: let's be the best, or the first, or the richest. This describes the space race between Elon Musk, Sir Richard Branson and Jeff Bezos. The drawback of going after a moonshot is that once you achieve it, that win can be taken from you the next day, so you have to compete again, and again. It sounds a bit exhausting, doesn't it?

---

*   If you decide to do the latter, you might find the tool called the *Wheel of Changes* useful. It was created by award-winning coach Marshall Goldsmith, and is designed for individuals to assess their current particular skills and behaviours, and therefore to plan their personal development. However, you may as easily apply it to your context. The wheel has two predominant axes: keep/change and positive/negative, which divide the wheel into four main quadrants: *creating* — the innovative quadrant of the wheel where you consider what you can add or invent; *eliminating* — this quadrant refers to the eradication or reduction of behaviours that are outdated, ineffective, or downright harmful; *accepting* — this quadrant is for the aspects that you need to delay or make peace with; and, finally, p*reserving* — in this quadrant you map what you need to improve or maintain. Doing this exercise will surface for you the challenges that lay ahead of the desired change to your context. In that way you will go into such a battle with your eye wide open.

A 'just cause' takes the opposite approach. You can see it as a continuous improvement that never ends, like regenerating our environment or eradicating injustice. Your 'just cause' may change focus as things improve along the way but the end-game doesn't exist, because a 'just cause' is not about individual winning and losing. It is about either everybody winning or about continuing the game.[50] Let's look again at the billionaires' space race. While I suspect that for Sir Richard Branson and Jeff Bezos it was a moonshot (almost literally), for Elon Musk, it is a very different game, as he seems to have a 'just cause' driving all his endeavours, which is to accelerate the advent of sustainable energy and to prolong the existence of the human race.[51] It doesn't matter if you win today because what you are striving for is not momentary success but the greatest possible progress in the desired direction, progress made by you, and by others alongside you. In this way, 'just cause' is a vision that is communal — because there is, for sure, more than one person who would like to see the future in a similar way as you see it.

What's more, people can subscribe to multiple 'just causes'. They can be as much supporters of activities leading to developing sustainable energy, stopping food waste, and elevating educational standards. For some of these causes, you might be a leader; in others, a contributor. In any case, you can verbalise it, argue it and most importantly, inspire others to join you in making this vision, this 'just cause', a reality.

Designing your vision

You can either create your vision and call others to join you in it, or you can join a vision of others (such as your organisation) and help others contribute to it. I am writing this because many leaders feel that just following their organisation's vision doesn't give them space for their own vision. This is a mistaken perspective. As a leader, you always have space to create a vision for yourself and your team. Yes, it might have some boundaries that are set by your organisation but it doesn't mean you don't have enough freedom to shape your part in the way you would like to.

Alternatively, you might find yourself in a scenario where your organisation doesn't have a vision that is in any way inspirational for either you or your team, or that various stakeholders have different visions that don't quite come together. In such a situation, you can formulate a mini-vision enveloping just one part of the organisation with the idea that when the time is right, this vision can become an inspiration for other stakeholders and other parts of the organisation and eventually grow to become the vision for everybody. This is a much harder path to take compared to the former scenario but I've seen it work and I've seen great leaders dedicating years for the vision they believed in to become embedded across the entire organisation.

Even if you decide to formulate a vision just for your team, it is worth both time and effort. Yes, maybe your organisation is not quite ready for it yet. Maybe it will never be ready. But you can always see it as, on the one hand, a great exercise in creating and working towards a cause that catches the hearts of yours and others and, on the other, it can become your litmus paper test for whether the context you find yourself in allows you to develop as a leader in a direction that you find desirable.*

In either situation, it is worth considering a few qualities of a powerful vision.[52] Firstly, it needs to be resilient. It means that your vision needs to withstand technological, cultural and political change. This is why a moonshot often fails as a long-lasting vision. Being the best in a given technology works for only as long as that technology remains on top. Being the biggest on the market can easily be shaken by a political shift, such as losing the position of providing your services for the government. If you can see any such force potentially negatively impacting your vision, it is an indication that perhaps you do not yet have a compelling 'just cause' to propel you.

Secondly, a vision needs to be inclusive. It needs to feel like an invitation. There is a famous story about NASA, where the janitors there would say they were helping to send people to the moon. This is the kind of inclusiveness I am talking about. I've seen many organisations where the accounting team, or the administrative team, or the HR team, felt like they were an external agency to the organisation they were a part of. Frankly, I've seen design departments that felt the same. There is little agency and little inspiration in that feeling. So, you can measure

---

*   Another option is to start even smaller and create a very local vision for you and your team that doesn't concern anybody else; for example, how great a team you can become.

whether your vision is truly inclusive if you can see that everybody, no matter what role they hold in the organisation, wants to be a part of it and feels that they can contribute.

Finally, your vision needs to be service-oriented. It means that the results of your actions should, first and foremost, benefit others. Imagine a psychotherapist whose only purpose in listening to your struggles is to make themselves feel better. I guess your first visit to them would be the last. Or imagine having a boss who gave you advice that would benefit them more than you (I had that boss, and it felt really bad when I realised the hidden reasons behind their words). So, if you set the vision to get more power or to get a promotion, it is a sign that this is not a vision, it is a selfish cause. But if you can honestly say that it benefits the world and your organisation including the people who work there, you are on the right track.

The sum of all visions

As I mentioned earlier, although your vision is not the same as your purpose, it has its roots in it. Imagine that you created such a vision by yourself. Would it inspire your team? It may. Sometimes people want to follow a great vision set by others. Think of Martin Luther King, Nelson Mandela or Greta Thunberg. But that doesn't mean they wouldn't like to chip into the creation of that vision so that they get a chance to have their purposes rooted in it too. This is why I am a great advocate of creating a vision together with others. When you decide to do it, you can start with a blank slate or you can bring your concept to the table. Either way, if you give space to everybody else to co-create the vision with you, not only will they be more motivated to follow it but also (or perhaps, above all) your vision will for sure become richer, more far-sighted and likely more daring (it is because you will gain a broader perspective about the possibilities that lay ahead). Even if, at the end of the day, the vision you proposed becomes the vision that is claimed as the one to pursue, you have managed to build your following simply because you made everybody else feel included.

It would seem like we are done here but there is one more aspect that is crucial. As inspirational as your vision might be, it aims at the impossible. This means that it can become a little abstract to live by from one day to the next. This is why it is worth adding some edges to it. Edges are the criteria that define how you want to pursue your vision. Imagine that you decide to climb Mount Everest. This is your vision. Now, you need to decide how you want to do it. Are you going to use the sherpas to help you get there or are you doing all of it on your own? Are you going to climb the South Col Route or the Northeast Ridge? Are you using oxygen? These constraints are your edges, the boundaries you are going to honour. You can decide whether you want to have your products, your processes, your interactions to be brave or modest, surprising or familiar, creative or analytical, and so forth. Working with edges will help you and your team keep on the track you chose. It will also make it easier to keep your vision in mind day after day and follow through with it. *

As much as you need a vision and edges for your team and organisation, it is also good to establish a vision and edges for your leadership style. Once again, the best vision is something that you will spend your whole life trying to reach but never quite get there. You might also want to define your edges for how you want to lead. Do you want to be an oasis of peace and calm or do you want to lead with energy and action? Do you want to be more practical or maybe more playful? Do you see yourself as a leader teaching others to be autonomous or would you rather see yourself as supportive of your team, or both? These are all questions that, on the one hand, help you understand how you want to contribute and, on the other, they enable you to better understand and therefore trust yourself as you keep developing as a leader.

Inspiring others

Defining an inspirational vision is a crucial aspect of any leadership practice. It helps our minds determine what we want to focus on. In order to do so effectively, you also need a narrative that explains that vision to others, so that they can see what you see. You might argue that you'd rather have goals, metrics, and key performance indicators (KPIs) than a narrative. However, while things like metrics and KPIs are a good idea, creating a persuasive narrative will get you much further when it comes to inspiring your team and your organisation,

---

* I explain in detail how to define your edges in my first book *The Umami Strategy.*[53]

and here's a reason why. Our cognitive system is tuned to see the world in narratives — we tell ourselves stories about everything that happens around us, we even dream in narratives. We are also evolutionarily susceptible to being influenced by the narratives of others. Think of the last piece of gossip you heard, or consider a recent political campaign. They are powerful narratives, for better or for worse. Why is this the case?

Any narrative carries with it enough ambiguity so that every person who hears it can make it their own. This ambiguity allows the narrative to be adjusted to any changes in the context. If your vision is about advancing sustainable energy, for example, there is certainly more than one way to get there, so you and your team have the space to adapt it flexibly as the situation evolves. The narrative also allows you to act small and still be a part of the story (like the NASA janitors).

There is one final value of using a narrative, before any metrics. Metrics seldom trigger a positive emotion by themselves, they are just too factual. They can make us feel as if we were back at school. There is a grading system and we need to make the grade in order to pass to another class or to graduate altogether.* Only a few people enjoy that system and see it as imaginary and inspirational. A powerful narrative has the opposite effect. It serves as a framework for action but the action within that frame is chosen by those who follow it. Furthermore, if your vision is a part of a bigger vision, a narrative allows you to depict both the entire picture and your particular fragment of that picture. But above all, a good story builds a sense of community because it becomes a story for all (including you). Of course, all this is true only once you, as a leader, first and foremost follow that vision. If this is not the case, the vision and a narrative that explains it will likely be seen as a claptrap, a story to make you look good on the outside but not a true inspiration to follow.**

---

*   When you operate solely based on metrics, goals, or key performance indicators, you might likely make others subconsciously feel as if you are treating them as children, not adults and partners.

**   As I am writing these words, I observe the reactions of the various companies to the war in Ukraine (2022). Many of them pride themselves to have great corporate values they live by. I must sadly say that in quite some cases, these values are apparently only good in a situation when the financial gain is secured (which in fact shows what the ultimate motivation for them is, doesn't it?)

WEEK

IV

CHALLENGE

This week's challenge will help you better understand your context so that you can identify how your stakeholders impact your vision and actions. You will also get some pointers on how to create a great vision and how to define your core qualities as a leader.

YOUR EXPERIMENT:
Describe it in a few sentences

Your deadline   ....

Positive observations			Negative observations
	√	✗	

Positive reactions			Negative reactions
	☺	☹	

Your conclusion ....

What to improve further? ....

CORE TASKS

1. Whenever you're trying to create change in any system, whether it's a piece of software, a group of people, or culture, you have to know where you are starting from. If you don't do that, you will likely flail around trying to find which levers cause which effects and that won't get you anywhere quickly. One way to gain such awareness is to draw a map of your organisation — not a traditional organisational chart but how it really works. Put yourself in the middle of that map and answer the following questions:

    Who has the power to say yes or no to you? ....
    ....

    Who is connected and dependent on whom in your surroundings?......
    ....

    Who is close to you, i.e. you affect them or you are being affected directly; who is further away? ....
    ....

    Who motivates the people who are truly in charge? What are their world views? ....
    ....

    As you look at this map, where can you see the space for you to act? What do you need to change in order to start creating the impact you want? Based on this analysis, can you see that the context in which you operate is promising? How can you make it more promising?

2. To define a powerful vision you need powerful questions to guide your thinking. Probably the most famous one is, "What business are we in?" asked by Theodore Levitt in his HBR article *Marketing Myopia*.[54] A question like this needs to be asked more than once. This is why the *Five Whys* exercise, popularised by Taiichi Ohno, an architect of the Toyota Production System, is probably the most often-used exercise during any strategic workshop. Here's my take on it to help you frame your ideas:

Answer the following questions:

- What value do we want to bring from the organisational perspective? Why is it important?
- What value do we want to bring from the people perspective (customers and employees)? Why is it important?
- What value do we want to bring from the perspective of the community we want to build? Why is it important?
- What value do we want to bring from the perspective of the entire society? Why is it important?
- What value do we want to bring from the perspective of the planet or the environment? Why is it important?

It may happen that you won't have answers to all these questions. That's ok. It is important to answer the first two because they express your organisational relevance. As for the following three, the answers you give represent your 'just cause'. Once you have captured the answers, write up your vision. You can do this by completing the following sentences:

We believe that ....
....

Therefore we commit ourselves to ....
....

In order to ....
....

3. In much the same way as you've just created the vision for your team or organisation, create a vision for your leadership. How do you want to lead? Write a manifesto for your leadership style. Remember to root it in your purpose.

I believe that ....
....

Therefore I commit to ....
....

In order to ....
....

EXTRAS

1. Define the edges for your leadership style. Are you going to be a leader who is like this or that? Choose these edges based on your strengths. It will be only natural to amplify what you are already good at. But at the same time dream big, dream about the leader you secretly want to become (even if it feels almost too scary to think about).

creative ———————————— analytical
practical ———————————— playful
serious ———————————— cheerful
active ———————————— calming
delicate ———————————— strong
enthusiastic ———————————— reflective
supportive ———————————— autonomous
energetic ———————————— quiet
proactive ———————————— reactive

Once you choose your core qualities, write down what they mean to you.

My first edge is ....
....
It means ....
....

My second edge is ....
....
It means ....
....

My third edge is ....
....
It means ....
....

2. Go back to the map you created in the first core exercise. Consider, who are your allies and who are the gatekeepers for your vision. They can be your colleagues, bosses, clients but also your family and even yourself (we tend to be our greatest gatekeepers, don't we?) Create a stakeholder map for your vision.[55]

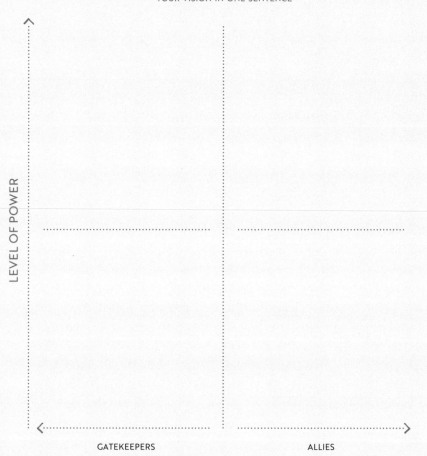

STAKEHOLDER MAP
YOUR VISION IN ONE SENTENCE

LEVEL OF POWER

GATEKEEPERS   ALLIES

Often when we think of our allies, we tend to assume their values and motivations are similar to ours and when we think about the gatekeepers, we see their values and motivations as very different from those that drive us. Select your three most crucial allies and three gatekeepers for your vision.

My allies	My gatekeepers
....	....
....	....
....	....

Consider each of them separately — what, do you think, drives them? Think about these drivers from three perspectives:

· Why would they want to support you? What motivates them?
· What are their fears? How can you alleviate them?
· What can they win or lose if they agree to your vision?

3. The manifesto you created about your vision is the basis for a narrative that you can share with others. But a manifesto may still not be as inspirational as you might hope for. A step further is to think of a metaphor that could explain your vision. What can you compare it to? Come up with two possible metaphors and share these with someone you trust. Ask them to help you make one of these metaphors even more powerful and convincing. Once you feel ready, perhaps it is a good moment to share it with your team. When you choose to do so, ask each of your team members to set one goal they could achieve in the next month that could progress the vision. Commit to these goals together and give it a try.

LOOKING BACK

You just completed one-third of this course. It is time to pat yourself on the back. As you celebrate, look back at the past week. How did it go? I can imagine that it was a hell of work to do. But this also means that you have a great vision of who you want to be as a leader based on your purpose, your strengths, and the idea of what the best version of you as a leader can be. Whatever you see, you are doing great!

Now, look more specifically back at the previous week:

1. How many core tasks did you manage to complete? How did they help you? Where were you stuck?

2. Did you run your experiment this week? What was it? What was the outcome? Was it noticed by others around you? Is it something you plan to continue with? Or perhaps you have another idea of how to alter and improve on it?

3. If you were to see what your greatest contribution was this week, what would it be? Why?

4. Was there anything else that resonated with you? What was it? Why do you think it was important? How does it help you define your unique leadership practice?

Defining Your Rhythm

No such thing as multitasking

The value of routines

Cadence and slack time

This week's challenge

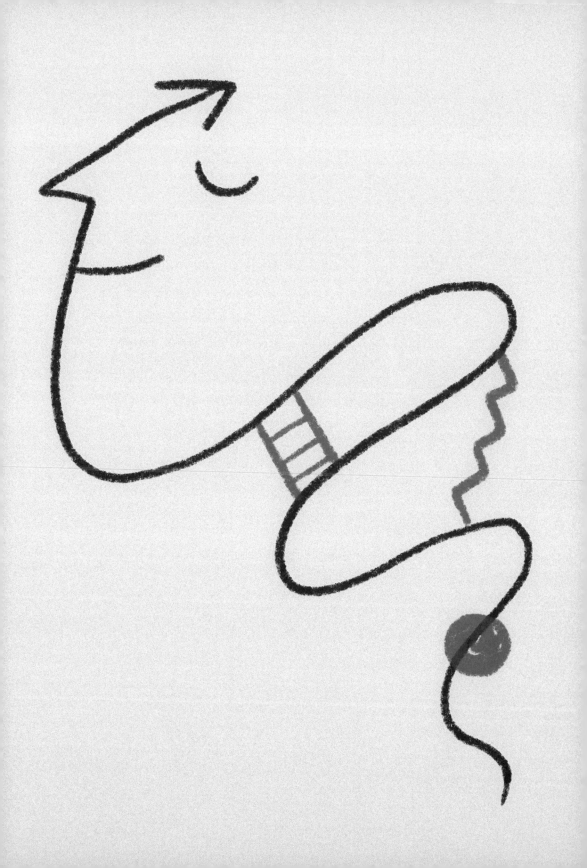

No matter how an organisation is managed in general,
as a leader you always have space to define your own rhythm.
Such rhythm is a repeatable, predictable pattern that
brings about your physical, emotional and mental comfort.
It combines firmness with flexibility and in this way
increases your chances for success, not only professionally
but personally, so that at the end of the day,
month or year, you are a happy, thriving person
rather than a tired and exhausted soul.

Work is a crucial part of life. We sleep with our phones next to our pillow, check new messages first thing in the morning, and allow ourselves to be interrupted by 'work' every minute of the day, regardless of whether it is working or leisure time. To remedy this, for decades, we were striving to achieve work-life balance. The idea behind this was to try to find an equilibrium between the demands of our careers and the demands of our personal life. It is an interesting concept in the sense that it seems to propose a clear-cut distinction between staying at the office and being at home. However, life keeps on proving to us to be more complicated than that — it does not easily succumb to such clear-cut rules, no matter how hard we might try. Fortunately, there is an alternative way of thinking about how we spend our days called *work-life integration.*

According to UC Berkeley's Haas School of Business, work-life integration is, "an approach that creates more synergies between all areas that define 'life': work, home, family, community, personal well-being, and health".[56] It means that, instead of setting hard boundaries between the different parts of your life, you approach the transitions between them as gentle pivots. It allows you to think of your day as something that can be flexibly shaped rather than rigidly set. But there is a slippery slope here. Since your work as a leader is never-ending, it is easy to fill in every second of your days with it at the cost of other parts of your life. In other words, there is a risk that your work becomes your life. Or, even if you try to combine the two, you might find yourself thinking about work while 'officially' doing something else. As Stephen Covey writes in *First Things First,* "Some of us get so used to the adrenaline rush of handling crises that we become dependent on it for a sense of excitement and energy".[57] It can become an addiction, where work excitement trumps anything else. And it often starts with falling into a trap of believing that we can multitask.*

No such thing as multitasking

We have four distinct types of memory. Our *working memory* is responsible for holding a mental representation of something that just happened for a few seconds. This is how we remember a phone number just long enough for us to type it into our phone. Then, we are equipped with *episodic memory* that records events in our daily life. The neurones involved in this process are responsible for encoding what happened, with whom, when, and how, and store that episode so that we can remember it later.** Next, there is *semantic memory,* our permanent knowledge, extracted from the parts of the brain responsible for episodic memory, generalised, and integrated into our general knowledge about the world.*** Finally, we have *procedural memory*, which gets activated when we repeat an activity over and over again (like driving a car or cycling). As you repeat that activity, neurones in your brain become more efficient, turning it into a routine that you can conduct without paying much attention to it.[58]

All these memory types are run by a part of our brain that neuroscientists call the *executive control*.[59] It is like a switchboard that orients, directs, and governs our mental processes much like, "a railroad yardman who tends the switches in the busy railway station and manages to bring each train to the right track by choosing the appropriate orientation for each switch".[60] It is one of the attention systems that activates mental operations appropriate for a given task while dampening all the others. It makes sure that the 'program' runs smoothly, detects errors, and is responsible for correcting the course of action if anything goes wrong.

There is a close connection between the *executive control* and your *working memory*. To be able to correctly execute a given task you need to constantly keep in mind all the elements that enable this task to happen (like the intermediate results, taken steps, tasks to be done, and so on).

---

*   Many leaders even appear to believe that they are master-multitaskers.

**   The episodic memory is one of our learning mechanisms.

***   This process typically happens while we sleep.

It controls the inputs and outputs that march through your conscious memory, also called the *global neural workspace*.[61] This space acts like a router deciding which piece of information should go where and in what order. These mental operations are slow and serial because the *global neural space* can process one piece of information at a time. Psychologists call this phenomenon *a central bottleneck*. There is a line of activities waiting to get your attention and if you are focused on one, you can't be simultaneously focused on another. This means that no multitasking is possible at this level of our mental structure. So, if you think you are a multitasker you are cheating yourself. Certainly, your brain is juggling a queue of information but it is always working on one piece at a time. Why then do so many of us seem to believe that multi-tasking is our unique skill? It is an illusion. If you'd like to test yourself you can do a little experiment.

Ask someone to play a high-pitched sound and show you a piece of paper with a letter written on it. Your job is to press a button with your left hand when you hear the sound and another one with your right hand when you see the letter. Things will go smoothly for as long as there is an equal (even if a very short) time interval between these two tasks. Problems begin when the sound is played at the same moment as the letter is shown to you. You will notice that the first task is done as quickly as before but the second is much slower. This proves that while your *central executive* is deciding to deal with the first task, the second needs to wait in line. And this lag is huge. On a simple task like this, it takes a few hundred milliseconds. Imagine now how much time your brain needs to switch between writing an email, talking to your colleague, and whatever the third task is you might be trying to do in parallel. The first stimulus is consciously processed, while the others need to wait to capture your attention once your *global neural workspace* is free to proceed. We don't perceive how much this waiting time takes, this is why we believe in the possibility of multitasking. If you still don't quite believe me, try this second experiment.

Take six sheets of paper and a timer. Your job is to tear each sheet into twenty pieces (don't worry about how even they are). Time yourself as you are tearing each sheet of paper. I am guessing, it takes you about thirty seconds, give or take. Now, take another set of six sheets.

Once again you need to tear each of them into twenty pieces. But this time your job is to first tear a batch of six pieces from every sheet before you repeat the procedure and tear the second and third batch of six pieces from every sheet again. Finally, you will have the last batch of four pieces per sheet to tear. Time yourself again to see how much time it takes you to tear a single piece of paper. You will realise that it most likely took you about three minutes. It is also quite likely that some sheets are torn not into twelve but into eighteen, nineteen, or twenty-one pieces.

This exercise shows three things. It reiterates that multitasking doesn't work. It demonstrates the delay in proceeding with the task caused by hitting the *central bottleneck* over and over again. Finally, it shows that while you pretend to be multitasking you are much more prone to making mistakes as your *episodic memory* doesn't have enough time to correct the possible errors. There is one additional thing that this experiment shows. While you pretend to multitask, rather than promptly delivering results on one task (of tearing one page into 20 pieces) after another, you delay them all and then release them almost at the same time.* What's the point?

As a leader, you might certainly be provoked to keep on trying to multitask by everything that is happening around you. Aren't you expected to communicate, make decisions, think strategically, solve problems, and do whatever else, all at the same time? But this is a trap that will eventually make you feel exhausted and ineffective. So, instead, play to the strengths of how your brain works, rather than against it. Sequence your activities to give your brain time to process the subsequent activities with as few errors as possible and without mental exhaustion. Over time, you will also become more efficient at doing what you are doing. This, in turn, may give you the illusion that you are multitasking again, but it is not so. It only means that you are becoming faster in switching between tasks with fewer errors. Having an order helps a lot in achieving this.

---

*   That is a different topic altogether, well worth paying attention to, though beyond the scope of this book.

The value of routines

Years ago, I went on a course to become a rescue diver. It took place in a tiny village, Andavadoka in Madagascar, thirty-six to seventy hours by car from the capital Antananarivo, and a three-hour helicopter flight to the nearest decompression chamber in Mauritius. The exam was preceded by an intense training led by a cheerful Australian instructor, Kirk. We practiced every day for more than two weeks. We had to learn how to pull a panicking person from underwater, how to drag an unconscious victim to the shore, and how to apply first aid. The daily challenges changed and we never knew what the next task would be. But we knew one thing. We had to be prepared. Our equipment needed to be checked and we had to be sure that we were not going to endanger ourselves while trying to help someone else. We kept practicing this preparation until it became a habitual routine in getting ready for a rescue action. And while the action itself was unpredictable, our preparation was highly structured.

This array of movements we went through every time — from making sure that our valves were open, checking if our regulators were providing air, to seeing how much air there was in our tanks (among many other tasks) — increased our ability to deal with the unpredictability of what we had to do. Yet, so many of us assume that when we find ourselves in an unpredictable situation, we are allowed spontaneous self-organisation. Such spontaneity, unfortunately, more often than not leads to disorganisation and is likely to cause us to fail or at least be less successful than we would hope for.

Routines are the tools aimed at reducing the energy consumption your brain requires to orient itself in a given situation. It is a powerful scaffolding for responding to whatever circumstances you find yourself in. Routines help you push some of the activities into your procedural memory — the one that gets activated when you repeat an activity over and over again. In that way, you create space for your brain to pay attention to whatever is going on that you haven't expected, while executing the lower level actions automatically. Routines also signal for you that a particular context demands from you and others certain ways of acting and reacting. For example, if you are a surgeon going into an operating theatre, the process of scrubbing up signifies the initiation of the surgery, where your identity aligns with the role you are about to perform, triggering attitudes that may not be your standard behaviour outside this context.*

But routines are not only about you. They are also a way to bring connectedness to your team. Routines reduce uncertainty, regulate emotions, create social connection and help to keep an eye on the performance and well-being of others.[63] They are the social glue of the culture you want to build. During my days at Google, we had weekly TGIF (which is short for Thank God, It's Friday) meetings on Friday at 5pm. The routine would start with the song *Heidi* being played from the speakers across the Zurich office. Most of us would come down to the cafeteria, where a little stage was created for our bosses to answer all questions we collectively voted as important during that week. Then we would have a little party to officially start the weekend.

Routinising parts of your work improves your focus, organisation and productivity, as routines offer a sense of control. What's more, successful routines lower stress levels whenever something unpredictable happens, as they anchor you in tasks and activities that you are familiar with. One thing that is crucial to remember: routines need to be systematically maintained. If you let them slip, they will be quickly abandoned. The very first step in doing this is to give your actions some cadence.

Cadence and slack time

Cadence can be seen as a rhythm, or a set of nested rhythms, that span weeks, months and even years. You might dedicate Mondays to planning and reviewing, Tuesdays to catching up on what's going on with your team members, Wednesdays for strategic work, and so on.

---

*   Many famous artists routinised their daily practice. For example, throughout the 1930s, the painter Joan Miró woke daily at 6am, bathed, ate a light breakfast, and then painted from 7am to noon. After that, he would leave his studio to exercise for an hour, be it gymnastics, boxing or jogging. Tim Ferris went so far as to create his morning routine based on hundreds of interviews he conducted on his podcast *the Tim Ferris Show* and then described in his book *Tools of Titans*.[62] These routines bring light structure to your day while keeping the connection with your purpose and intentionality of your actions.

I am talking days here but you might think of it in different blocks of time (like half-days or half-weeks). You can even expand it over a longer time if the different periods in the year of your organisation have their rhythm (such as product launches, freezes, etc). Your cadence can flexibly change over time, of course. But even with some fluctuations, it gives you more peace of mind and those who work with you a sense of when you will be available for them. It also allows you and everybody else to plan their days and to have the space to focus on their work-life integration.

There is a trap when building your cadence, that so many of us fall into. Sooner or later, we find ourselves filling our schedule up to its brim because we feel that if we are not busy we are not performing well enough. In an interview available on YouTube, Bill Gates mentions his conversation with Warren Buffett about keeping busy.[64] When Microsoft was becoming highly successful Gates saw having a calendar filled up as a sign of being indispensable. Buffett showed Gates his agenda, where days (and sometimes even weeks) were free. It was his way of giving himself time to think, to learn and to strategise. It made Bill realise that he was allowing others to run his agenda and that he was busy with the *urgent* rather than *important*. Gates commented, "It's not a proxy of your seriousness that you filled every minute of your schedule". Buffett summed up that, "Busy is the new stupid" — because at the end of the day time is the only thing you are not able to get more of.*

So, here's a question for you: are you ruling your agenda or is your agenda ruling you? If you find yourself overbooked, you could rethink your current cadence and drop activities that are not your priorities. If this is not enough you could, for example, plan your activities

---

* I remember the first time I got my agenda and my email inbox cleared. I practically went into a state of panic. For once, I didn't quite know what to do with all this time I suddenly had on my hands. And I felt as if I was not needed anymore. My default reaction was to get back to busying my schedule and filling my days with whatever came first. Even today, I sometimes allow my agenda and my inbox to rule my day. But as the practice of meaningful scheduling grew on me, I am less and less inclined to do so, finally having time to do things I would otherwise never have the mental energy to do.

as large blocks. Or, if needed, you might want to add extra time after each meeting so you can immediately plan or execute some of the actions you just discussed, rather than have to remember what was said later on. Larger blocks of time for one activity mean fewer context switches and, therefore, less cost in energy your brain needs to deal with all of it.[65]

Within your agenda you also need to find space for slack time. Slack time is nothing more than time available between the different actions you perform. It looks like time for doing nothing. Doing nothing? Seriously? Not quite. It is time for the activities that border on your professional and personal life such as working on the tasks from this book. It is also time to unwind and to switch contexts. If you feel guilty about creating space for slack time during your working hours ask yourself this — should activities that you plan for it consume the time you would otherwise have for yourself, family and friends?

You must, however, be mindful not to turn your slack time into catch-up time for finishing things rather than for your professional development. If you find yourself in the need to constantly catch up during your slack time, you still have too much on your plate and in your agenda. Slack time is for thinking, and thinking ahead is absolutely at the core of a leader's job. This is the only (or one of the very few) tasks you cannot delegate.

WEEK

CHALLENGE

You've already started working on your work-life integration last week when you defined what edges you would like to have as a leader. They indicate what working style would likely fit you best. Let's build on that. First, take a look at what activities keep you busy. It is important to have such a reflection to consciously capture your current practice before you begin to change it. Once you get that picture, try to make it into a desired one and see what you need to change to get there.

YOUR EXPERIMENT:
Describe it in three sentences

Your deadline ....

Positive observations   Negative observations

✓ ✗

Positive reactions   ☺ ☹   Negative reactions

Your conclusion...

What to improve further? ....

CORE TASKS

1. Look back over the past month. If you were to assess how much time you spent on the following activities, what would it look like?

    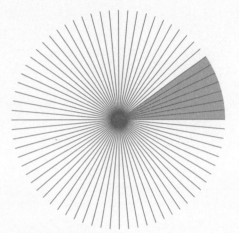

    - Working with strategy
    - Working with people
    - Working with content
    - Education of self and others
    - Enabling and coaching
    - Playing politics
    - Sitting in meetings
    - Evangelising
    - Recuperating
    - Other

    If you marked 'other', what falls into that category?

    The activities represented on this wheel don't have to be evenly distributed, the wheel can be lopsided depending on the leadership practice you are designing for yourself. There are, however, four possible warning signals. One, if you find yourself spending too much time with content. You are a leader, not an expert, so if you do the expert work, it might be a sign that either you have a hard time letting go of the actual content, or you are not trusting your team enough. The second warning signal is when you have a lot of time dedicated to 'other' activities. This might mean that you are spreading yourself thin on activities that are not the core of your leadership role. The third is when you spend your days playing politics and sitting in meetings. Meetings and politics are an unavoidable part of a leadership role but if they dominate your days, it might mean that the context you are operating in is unfavourable or that other people rule your agenda. The final warning sign regards recuperating for too long. This can be a sign of experiencing imposter syndrome, mental exhaustion or even the beginnings of burnout.

2. Look at the past week and draw a calendar view of how much time you
    spent on each type of activity that landed in your wheel.

MON	TUE	WED	THU	FRI	SAT	SUN

- Is each activity rendered in long blocks of time or are you jumping
  from one activity to another?

- Who rules your agenda — you or others? If others, who are they?

- How does it make you feel to keep your agenda like this? What is
  the upside? What is the downside?

3. Now think about what your agenda could ideally look like. Draw
    an example of it for the next week. Keep in mind that multitasking
    doesn't exist and that you are striving for work-life integration. Remem-
    ber to add slack time. As you are looking at this ideal agenda, how does
    it make you feel? How realistic is it? What is more and what is less real-
    istic about it? What could be the first step towards making it happen?

4. Write your work manifesto. How would you like to work? What are your
    non-negotiable boundaries? What are your routines and your cadence?
    How can you include slack time? Share your manifesto with others on
    your team. Encourage them to write their manifestos too. If you feel
    like it, print it out and hang it on the wall so that you are reminded of
    your own working rules.

EXTRAS

1. Consider a longer period of time (a quarter or a year). Is there a cadence dictated by your organisation that you can see? Maybe there are product launches, freezes, windows for marketing campaigns, or other repeatable events. Map them out. How do they impact the work of your team or organisation? How do they impact your rhythm? How can you improve it based on what you see?

JAN	FEB	MAR	APR	MAY	JUN

JUL	AUG	SEP	OCT	NOV	DEC

2. Design a morning routine for yourself. Create it deliberately so you delay getting pulled into work.* Try your routine out and see if it suits you. You may not be able to carry such a routine out fully every day but try to do some elements of it and then adjust the routine to better fit you.

3. As the last task this week, think of and describe one tiny team routine. You may think of it yourself or you can ask your team members to help you out. Once you have it, give it a try.

---

*   One practice I do is to write each morning an *Intention for the Day*, something that will guide my actions as the day progresses.

LOOKING BACK

This week was about action in the real world. Things are becoming tangible. The action starts taking place. Take a look at the past week. How did it go? Did it change the way you plan your time? As you are thinking of the sheer amount of change you are facing (which might get scary), what would you *give yourself an A* for? You now know a way in which you want to shape your time and the way you act. This is something that will stay with you and keep on delivering on ideas, long after you have completed this course.

Now, look more specifically back at the previous week:

1. How many core tasks did you manage to complete? How did they help you? Where were you stuck?

2. Did you run your experiment this week? What was it? What was the outcome? Was it noticed by others around you? Is it something you plan to continue with? Or perhaps you have another idea of how to alter and improve on it?

3. What was your best idea or your 'aha'-moment this week? Why?

4. Was there anything else that resonated with you? What was it? Why do you think it was important? How does it help you define your unique leadership practice?

Expanding Your Worldview

*Remember the gorilla experiment from Week 3,
the one where you missed a chest-pounding gorilla while
you were busy counting how many shoots a black team took?
Such blindness happens because humans are pattern-seekers,
so we tend to look for things we expect to find. But if you do
indeed notice only 5% of what happens around you,
how can you comprehend what's really going on?
The only way to do so is to create a team around you that sees
what you don't see. If you don't expand your worldview,
you run the risk of doing more of the same over and over again.
But if you create an environment that embraces diversity
with enough common ground, bam! Innovation happens.*

Groupthink*

If you ever organised a focus group session with a fairly homogenous group, you most likely saw how quickly and inevitably participants' opinions converged into one, reaching not necessarily the most insightful, but the safest conclusion. And if you ever remained silent in a meeting because you felt you were wrong, or you were afraid that your ideas were stupid, or it looked like everyone else had an opinion different from yours, you fell prey to the phenomenon of groupthink. The concept of groupthink was discussed as early as the 1970s by Irving Janis, and has since been proven over and over again as a terrible practice in all sorts of contexts, ranging from business to design and politics, and can have terrible consequences such as in the case of the attack on Pearl Harbour.[66, 67]

Before Pearl Harbour was attacked on December 7th 1941, American intelligence had intercepted messages indicating a pending Japanese strike in the Pacific. The Pearl Harbour command received several warning messages about it but following group discussions between Army and Navy officers, a conclusion was drawn that the attack was unlikely. There were two main reasons for this. One was the assumption that Japan would only attack after being attacked, and the other was that even if the attack should happen, they would be able to detect and destroy the attackers before they reached the harbour. The officers overestimated the power of their country (which caused them to fail to prepare), and believed themselves to be in the right, and therefore ignored the consequences of their actions (or non-actions in this case).

---

*   I am curious whether you noticed how I broke the scheme of chapter construction for this week. What reaction did it invoke in you? This is probably the reaction you typically have when a pattern you expected in suddenly absent.

They used rationalisations to ignore the warning signs and stereotyped the Japanese army as being too weak and scared to attack the US base. Finally, pressure towards uniformity must have played a role in a hierarchical structure of the army where the opinions of those higher up were seen as more informed, and therefore wiser.

According to Janis, when we succumb to groupthink, we tend to overestimate our group and its capabilities. We think we are invulnerable, and we don't question the morality of the group itself and the conclusions it arrives at, especially if our knowledge of the subject matter is somewhat limited. (On the other hand, those among us who know more tend to underestimate our own knowledge and ability).* Furthermore, we tend to rationalise our joint way of thinking. We fall into a trap of assuming that our opinions are representative of everyone 'in their right mind', and ignore those who are underrepresented, so, in other words, we are prone to ignore minority opinions. As if this wasn't bad enough, in any groupthink situation we experience pressure towards uniformity. The most common manifestation of such a feeling is when you are reluctant to speak up if you feel that everyone else's opinion is different from yours. This happens especially in situations when you feel that others are more powerful than you or if you don't hold strong opinions, giving the group a sense that silence is a form of agreement while in actuality it is a form of self-censorship, creating only an illusion of unanimity.

---

*   This is known as the Dunning–Kruger effect: a cognitive bias stating that people with low ability at a task overestimate their own ability, and that people with high ability at a task underestimate their own ability.

How many people in your professional life have tried to convert other people to their point of view without recognising the lost time, money, and engagement involved in this fruitless endeavour? Group-think means that, instead of seeing more of what's going on around you, you keep on seeing the same 5% you see anyway. But while groupthink is deeply flawed, it is also proven that individual intuition is too often wrong, and group intuition is uncannily accurate.[68] How come?

The wisdom of a diverse crowd

A former Polish prime minister is said to have run a small council. This council comprised people who held opinions and worldviews ranging from extremely liberal to extremely conservative. Whenever there was a difficult decision to make, the PM would present the challenge at hand to this council and listen to the sometimes fierce discussions. The goal was not to reach consensus. It was to trigger a variety of responses as an exercise in broadening his perspective. It was a way for him to see things he wouldn't otherwise, because they didn't fit the pattern he would naturally be looking for. What the PM practiced is known as the *wisdom of a crowd* phenomenon.[69]

How does the wisdom of a crowd differ from groupthink? In the book *Superforecasting, The Art and Science of Prediction,* Philip Tetlock tells the story of the Cuban conflict of 1961 under John F. Kennedy's presidency (also known as the Bay of Pigs invasion), which was later dissected by various historians who agreed that it was a plan created by presidential advisors under conditions of groupthink.[70] It led to keeping the entire mission as an independent action of anti-Castro guerrilla forces, to leak such information to the public and to have no contingency plan for recovering the American troops in the case of failure. Much like during the attack on Pearl Harbour, it was an example of "members of a small cohesive group that tended to maintain *esprit de corps* by unconsciously developing a number of shared illusions and related norms that interfere with critical thinking and reality testing".[71]

After the invasion fiasco, Kennedy ordered a post-mortem in order to understand how so many people could have been so wrong. As you might have already guessed, the analysis identified groupthink along with comfortable unanimity as the prime problem. The recommended remedy was scepticism. The idea was to question everything, invite external advisors to play the role of devil's advocate with no regard for authority and hierarchy. Kennedy himself would often leave the room to support free discussion, knowing that his presence, often unintentionally, affected the ongoing conversations. The advisors were expected to come up with multiple alternatives to choose from, each with their pros and cons (not just two or three, but ten or more). In this way, the group process in the White House radically changed from falling prey to groupthink to applying the wisdom of a crowd, leading to decisions such as not starting a nuclear war with the Soviet Union.[72]

This story shows how dangerous groupthink can be. The problem lies in the fact that groups that go too well together have a tendency to stay mellow, which means that they are not well inclined to question assumptions or face uncomfortable facts. They tend to believe that if everybody agrees with everybody else, they are all on the right track because they can't all be wrong, can they? If such 'easy to reach agreement' takes place, you may consider adding a disclaimer to the result stating that the fact you came to one single conclusion is a strong indicator that the group possibly doesn't have the appropriate mix to discuss the given topic. Fortunately, the right mix of people in a team can sharpen judgment and reach conclusions no one person would ever be able to reach. So, how can you foster group conversations without allowing them to slip into complacency?

As Aristotle said, "It is possible that the many, though not individually good men, yet when they come together may be better, not individually but collectively, than those who are so, just as public dinners to which many contribute are better than those supplied at one man's cost".[73] When you want to notice what you may not otherwise see, you need to gather a group of people with different, often contradictory opinions and either create the conditions for a safe exchange of their views among them, or collect their individual stories and look at the differences among these stories.* To do so well, however, you need just enough alignment among them so that you are not being led astray.

Just enough alignment

You might think that having a vision should be sufficient to provide alignment but, unfortunately, this is not the case. With just enough tendency to complacency, a vision is likely to become nothing more than a stack of platitudes and a recipe for groupthink under the umbrella of cosy agreement. If you strive for a broad picture you need to give voice

---

* One way to do so is by applying a *ritualised conflict*. It is a term for an artificial conflict that typically consists of three phases: *separation, transition,* and *incorporation*. Separation means that you leave the regular social world and its values and norms. You are allowed to behave in ways that are non-normative in a daily context (for example, you can apply humour and jokes as a way to get your point across). *Transition* indicates a state of ambiguity when you no longer hold your traditional status. The titles don't matter and everybody has an equal say regardless of their position in the team or experience. It is a little like entering a parallel universe where you are allowed to act in new ways using your hidden superpowers. The final phase, *incorporation,* is the moment when you connect whatever happened during the *ritualised conflict* with reality leading to a decision or action. A *ritualised conflict* is a great tool to get the best out of diverse teams without risking groupthink and complacency on the one hand, and an expression of unwanted behaviours such as aggression and general assholeness on the other.

to the outliers who see what you don't see, people who overlap with you rather than have a similar perspective to yours. Such an attitude is well captured in the words of Philip Tetlock addressing the forecasters he collaborated with:

> "Be cooperative but not deferential. Consensus is not always good; disagreement is not always bad. If you happen to agree, don't take this agreement — in itself — as proof that you are right. Never stop doubting. Pointed questions are as essential to a team as vitamins are to the human body. On the other hand, the opposite of group-think — rancour and dysfunction — is also a danger. Team members must disagree without being disagreeable".

One great way to encourage diversity in perspectives is captured by Edward de Bono's concept of the different thinking hats we can all assume in a given conversation.[74] De Bono argued that each one of us should try to take different positions in a discussion. He used a metaphor of hats of different colours to indicate a role you might be assuming at a given moment. The green 'creative' hat represents creative thinking. When you are 'wearing' this hat, your role is to explore a range of ideas and possible ways forward. The red 'emotional' hat represents feelings and instincts without having to justify them with logical arguments. With the yellow 'optimist' hat, you look at issues in the most positive light possible. You accentuate the benefits and the added value that could come from your ideas. When you get hold of the 'white hat' you become the team analyst discussing the facts and data, sharing background information and raising questions. The black 'judge' hat is about being cautious and assessing risks. You employ critical judgment and explain exactly why you have concerns. And the blue hat, also termed 'the conductor's hat' means that you manage the decision-making process. You have an agenda, ask for summaries, and reach conclusions.

Now, consider how these different perspectives can be multiplied when you have people with differing worldviews at the table. Yes, the conversation is going to take more time and most likely will be far more animated than in the case of cosy agreement. But the outcome you arrive at has a higher probability of being a truly informed decision leading to innovative solutions rather than the product of cosy agreement under the groupthink that most likely aims to maintain the status quo. There is one indispensable ingredient that is necessary in order to have a conversation like this: empathy.

Is empathy enough?

In a conversation on the *Catching the Next Wave* podcast, Yuan Wang, a leadership coach for women and people of colour, said, "Embracing diversity is not about being invited to the party. It is about being invited to dance".[75] Most of us at one time or another have found ourselves being almost 'in' but not quite. I can imagine you are able to empathise with that feeling. But is empathy enough?

Dr Brenè Brown defines empathy as taking the other person's perspective with the other's life circumstances in view in so far as you can grasp those circumstances.[76] It requires from you the ability to recognise a perspective of another person as their truth. It also requires acknowledging their emotions while staying out of judgement. In other words, it is about deeply listening without feeling either superior or protective of the other person. Empathy is a choice that calls for vulnerability and restrain from action. It is about walking alongside another person while they are going through whatever is happening in their lives.

Why would then empathy ever be bad? In the book *Against Empathy*, Paul Bloom draws an argument that it may be particularly important if you try to embrace diversity.[*,77] He shows that empathy we typically experience especially in a professional setting tends to be *shallow* rather than *deep*. Shallow empathy means that we are trying to see the world through someone else's eyes, or to read their emotions. We approach it as a cognitive task, much like strategising or solving problems and,

---

* Bloom defines empathy as "the act of coming to experience the world as you think someone else does." He builds on the more broadly known definition of empathy stated by Adam Smith, "the ability to walk a mile in other people's shoes". What Adam Smith was talking about is something known as *emotional empathy*, much like what you probably felt when you imagined yourself being excluded from a party. There is another kind of empathy known as *cognitive empathy*, which doesn't require you to feel what the other person feels, but to imagine what they might be going through (something I mentioned during Week 2 when sharing with you the story of Gareth, the school director).

as a consequence, we may not necessarily feel inclined to do anything. Conversely, deep empathy can be defined as the capability not just to imagine but to feel what others are experiencing.

> "It's the ability to actually enter the 'mind space' of another person so that you can sense their feelings and emotions. In a sense, your identity merges with theirs. The separateness between you and them fades away. Your 'self-boundary' melts away, so that in a sense — or to an extent — you become them."[78]

Once you experience such deep empathy it becomes impossible for you to make others suffer, as it would feel like you were harming yourself.* Shallow empathy, on the other hand, at best means that someone is willing to listen to another person but unlikely to act to resolve the problem they are facing and at worst that they exploit the weaknesses of another person to their advantage.**

Empathy also serves poorly whenever there is a larger number of people who need help, especially when their interests are contradictory. Imagine yourself standing in front of five conflicted team members, each of them with a different view on what happened and who the guilty party is. You may try to get into the shoes of one or two of them, but five? What typically happens in such situations is that you are likely to empathise more with those who were kind towards you in the past, who you enjoy collaborating with, and who you like the most. And with whom are we most likely to connect? With the people who are like us.

---

* If you kept on constantly feeling everyone's pain, your emotional state would be far from able to deliver calmness and assuredness to those around you. If you think about it, would you prefer a leader who is feeling your distress, or one who is calm in the face of a difficult situation? Would it be better if they were confident when you were anxious and able to see the bigger picture when you fall into the trap of narrow thinking? I guess your answer is, hell yeah. The same most likely holds for your team.

** Or it can be even worse. According to the psychologist Paul Gilbert, shallow empathy is what makes torture possible. Without it, a torturer would have no idea of the possible suffering they can cause. As they can 'put themselves in another person's shoes' they know that they are causing pain.

Such an inclination is called *empathy bias* and it basically means that we tend to empathise with those similar to us rather than those who we see as different.[*,79] Our brain betrays us in that way by responding to those we recognise as a part of our group rather than a group that we don't identify ourselves with. And, not long after you find yourself surrounded by people like yourself, while alienating the outliers who are crucial if you'd like to avoid groupthink and leverage the wisdom of a diverse crowd. This is why exercising empathy alone as a part of your leadership practice runs the risk of making you look for group homogenisation, rather than embracing diversity. Consider this — embracing inclusivity is an activity, not an attitude, that you must invest energy in. Therefore, you need a broader approach of compassion to fully embrace the advantages of diversity in your team.

*   Researchers from the University of Pennsylvania, MIT, and Harvard investigated what empathy bias might cause in people who feel a strong sense of belonging with a group.[80] They looked at three different social groups: Americans regarding people from the Middle East, Hungarians regarding Muslim refugees, and Greeks regarding Germans. The results showed that participants from all three countries showed significant empathy bias for their own groups. Experiencing such bias also suggested lower willingness to support the other group, either through charity or by inducing passive harm (such as refusing to provide aid during a terror attack).

WEEK

VI

CHALLENGE

We will further unpack the notion of compassion and its consequences next week. This week's challenge is about helping you to get a comprehensive picture of how diverse your team is and to provoke you to embrace the different perspectives in a more conscious and deliberate manner.

YOUR EXPERIMENT:
Describe it in three sentences

Your deadline ....

Positive observations   Negative observations

✓ ✗

Positive reactions   ☺ ☹   Negative reactions

Your conclusion ....

What to improve further? ....

CORE TASKS

1. Archetypes are the representations of behaviours and ways of thinking, that embody fundamental characteristics of a person. The most well-known definition probably comes from Carl Jung, who saw archetypes as a collectively-inherited unconscious idea, a pattern of thought or an image that is universally present in individual psyches. We can find archetypes in the descriptions of the gods and goddesses of Greek mythology and in the modern day Dilbert cartoon. Archetypes manifest in families, and each person in the group can recognise some aspect of themselves in each archetype.

   Try to create your own archetype.
   - What are your strengths and weaknesses?
   - What are your passions and dislikes?
   - What is your bright and dark side?
   - How would you call your archetype?

2. Create a family of archetypes for your team members. What are their strengths and weaknesses? What is their bright and dark side? What are their attributes and tools they use? How would you call their archetypes? Which of them are similar to your archetype and which are different? How would you order them according to how alike and how different they are from you? What strikes you as you go through this exercise?

   These are examples of the possible team archetypes to inspire your thinking.

THE INNOVATOR	THE CHANGE CATALYST	THE BUILDER	THE TRANSACTOR

THE PROCESSOR	THE COACH	THE COMMUNICATOR

3. Now that you know what archetypes your team members represent, think which of your blind spots each person can help you with.

   • What things can they see that you don't see?
   • What patterns are they sensitive to that you are not?
   • Are there any other blind-spots of yours that are not covered by your team members?
   • What archetypes could you add to your team to address these?

4. Design your own council, a council that will keep you on your toes and offer you the wisdom of a diverse crowd.

   • Who should sit there (from within and also from outside of your team)?
   • How often do you want to meet?
   • How do you meet?
   • How would you like to you design interactions between your council members?

EXTRAS

1. Once again, take a look at your team. Each member has a collection of amazing knowledge and skills. What is the hidden knowledge and skill in each of them, stemming from their hobbies, previous jobs and passions? What knowledge and skill do they have that you are not currently using? How can you make use of it in the future?

2. It is time to entertain issues you may not pay much attention to otherwise. This is a way to deepen your empathy towards your team. Draw a weekly timeline for each of your team members. What are they busy with? What are they struggling with? What makes them happy? What strikes you as you go through this exercise?

3. Spend some time working on something you like outside of your work (it can be a hobby or just a nice way to spend time). Use it as a way to explore how it is to learn and expand your perspectives outside of your work environment.

LOOKING BACK

You are halfway through this course. Your practice is changing radically by now. Take a look back over the last six weeks. How does it make you feel? What has changed? What are you more confident about? What still bothers you? What makes you feel proud?

Now, look more specifically back at the previous week:

1. How many core tasks did you manage to complete? How did they help you? Where were you stuck?

2. Did you run your experiment this week? What was it? What was the outcome? Was it noticed by others around you? Is it something you plan to continue with? Or perhaps you have another idea of how to alter and improve on it?

3. What will you give yourself an A for as you are heading towards the second part of this course?

4. How does Rule No 6 work for you? How can you further implement it into your life?

5. Was there anything else that resonated with you? What was it? Why do you think it was important? How does it help you define your unique leadership practice?

Building Trust

Early in the 20th century, being a trustworthy leader
largely meant providing explicit rules and policies.
Those times seem to be long gone. Today, a leader is
like a captain navigating the high seas full of hidden rocks,
wrecks and sudden storms without many tools
that aid them on that journey. So, for one, you need
a strong sense of direction. Then, you need to have the trust
of your crew so that they stay with you as you follow
that direction. If you want to build a team that journeys
alongside you through the high and low, you need
to embrace trust as a long term commitment.
Such a commitment begins with compassion.

ntil recently, empathy and compassion were seen as similar concepts. However, research shows that they differ in how they manifest — while empathy is just about being able to see the perspective of another (with all the shortcomings that might come with it, some of which I mentioned last week), compassion is defined by the desire to take action.[81] Such a desire is deeply evolutionary: helping others benefits us by strengthening the group we belong to, and opens the door to reciprocity. This is why compassion creates stronger connections between people, raises levels of trust, and enhances loyalty much more than empathy alone.[82]

Brains regulate each other

What we experience with and from others influences our experience of the world. Our breathing synchronises with those around us, our hearts beat in the same rhythm, we mirror each other's movements and facial expressions. Changes in one person's emotional state influence the emotions of those around them.* Such a phenomenon happens because we make energy deposits into and withdrawals from other people's *body budgets*. The metaphor of *body budgeting* comes from the book *How Emotions Are Made*, where professor Lisa Feldman Barrett uses it to explain how our brain allocates the energy in our body to keep us alive and well. To ensure that we keep our body budget in balance, the brain anticipates the body's needs and tries to satisfy them even before the need arises. For example, if you raise your voice, or even

---

*   If you ever experienced a sudden change of atmosphere in the room after somebody entered (or left), you know what I am talking about. There are people we like to be around and there are those known as 'energy vampires'. They suck our motivation and enthusiasm. Some are even the psychological equivalent of a black hole. When they are near you find it difficult to think.

make an unhappy face, you are most likely affecting what's going on in the brains and bodies of those around you, which means that they may not be so keen to spend time in your company in the future.

On the other hand, if you act in a compassionate way, your team feels respected, trusted and cared about. As a consequence, they tend to seek more interactions with you, because these interactions stimulate chemical reactions in their bodies that, on a basic level, make all of you feel good. So, the way you and others behave builds or destroys your openness towards honest and joyful interactions. This is why the job of a leader is to act in a compassionate way so that the body budgets of your team are well managed, which subsequently leads to *the social multiplayer effect* (commonly captured through the phrase 'what goes around comes around') allowing for the creation of a great team culture.[83] Professor Feldman Barrett sums this up by saying, "When people work in an environment where they can learn to trust each other, they will have less burden on their body budgets, saving resources that can be invested in new ideas".[84]

Trust or not to trust?

You might have heard the Machiavellian saying, "One ought to be both feared and loved, but as it is difficult for the two to go together, it is much safer to be feared than loved, if one of the two has to be wanting".[85] Anyone who adheres to this maxim shows mistrust.[*] A mistrusting leader doesn't believe that people can be efficient and deliver quality on their own, nor they are capable of being loyal without punishment or reward. Such leaders assume others to be driven by selfish intentions making them incapable of acting towards a common good.

Control and trust are incompatible because trust requires the freedom to make decisions and to act in ways that may not necessarily mirror the way the leader imagines or wishes. If you trust people, you believe

---

[*] Niccolò Machiavelli was a political philosopher and statesman, secretary of the Florentine Republic in the XV century, whose most famous work, *the Prince (Il Principe)*, brought him a reputation as an atheist and an immoral cynic. It is worth adding that he claimed that his experience and reading of history showed him that politics have always been played with deception, treachery, and crime.

that they are able to understand what is expected of them and deliver on that expectation to their best ability, and you accept that the steps they take to achieve this will be different from those you envisaged yourself.

Mistrusting leaders often assume that the intentions, behaviours and actions of others are sinister and harmful. They anticipate failure, and any deviation from their expectations is easily seen as such. To avoid failure, a mistrusting leader is inclined to practice micro-management. A need for control is closely linked to a need for power in the sense of hierarchical authority.* The most dangerous version of such power is power without responsibility. It leads to the development of a privileged mindset, where someone steps into that position without consideration of the impact their actions have on the people they are supposed to lead.** But even if one has power equipped with responsibility, a culture shaped by power becomes one that uses authority to compel others to follow its leaders by whatever means available.***, [87] Such an approach creates an atmosphere of fear, where independent thinking is seen as threatening. People who are managed by control and power know that they have to keep their heads down and reduce

---

*   The need for control often evokes *cordial hypocrisy*, "the strong tendency of people in organisations, because of loyalty or fear, to pretend that there is trust when there is none, being polite in the name of harmony when cynicism and distrust are active poisons, eating away at every existence of the organisation".[86]

** Such an attitude is otherwise known as *denial of denial*. It is a posture of blindness, much like a brick wall surrounding one's world so tightly it is impossible to penetrate. Their truth is the only truth and anyone who disagrees is wrong. Whatever happens is someone else's fault. Such a posture creates rigidity and a dominance that potentially becomes abusive because it denies anyone the right to hold a different point of view. The concept of *denial of denial* eliminates empathy and compassion, or even the ability to consider another point of view as valid. What is being denied doesn't exist for the denier, even when others can often very clearly see what's being denied. There is no space for difference, for reflection. Think of Donald Trump as an example of *denial of denial*.

*** April K. Mills contrasts this approach with "a powerful way of creating change that is present in all successful change efforts, but is never named distinctly for the force that it is. It is when a change agent chooses a change for themselves and then clears the obstacles for others to choose that change too".[88]

their actions to the minimum to lower their chances of being punished.[89] This leads to a loss of motivation, creativity, and loyalty, and stimulates an opportunistic attitude, where some seize chances to get ahead, while shifting blame for any mistakes on to others.

Certainly, there are important cultural differences in the way the relationship between a leader and their team is formed.[90] Regardless, if you are a mistrusting leader your team members are likely to become circumspect, ask for formal confirmation before they act (which costs you time and energy) and your ability to lead effectively will be damaged. This is because trust is built on a sense of obligation between you and your team. Trusting means believing that you all express good intentions and will act in your shared interest. It is based on the realisation that your way of doing things may neither be obvious to someone else with different background and history nor it may be the best way to act in absolute terms. In other words, the more you say, 'do it this way', the more you fail as a trusting leader. Micro-managing will lead to your team increasingly doing things behind your back or not doing them at all, and you will be presented with 'done deals' rather than invited to discussions. Before long, you find yourself in a vicious cycle of mistrust, control and exercising power. So, no matter how scary it may feel, you need to learn to trust — first yourself, then others.

How trust works

Trust is a social glue; the magic ingredient that is so hard to capture and yet one of the most important aspects that differentiates a successful team from one that struggles. Once you choose to trust, it is worth remembering that trust is reinforced by trusting. If you decide to trust, you seek proof that a person is worthy of that trust and usually, you are able to find it. The same holds for mistrust. If you decide not to trust, you will find evidence to reinforce that — you will be focusing on these aspects of behaviour that confirm your suspicions. It is worthwhile to remember that a person who is trusted tends to act in ways that are trustworthy, while a distrusted person might simply act out.

Dawid Wiener, a psychiatrist, cognitivist and philosopher, sees developing trust as a process shifting from the pragmatic to the more emotionally charged trust. You start by deciding to trust. It is nothing more than a calculation based on your hope that the other person has the qualities that enable them to 'earn' that trust, such as transparency in communication, fulfilment of duties and an adequate level of professionalism. Once a person proves trustworthy, you start predicting that if your trust was not broken in the past, there is a chance it won't be broken in the future either.[*] Such a person is earning a reputation: you begin to trust their capabilities and competence based on the consistency of how they act, rooted in goodwill, honest reactions and their consistency in action.

Then you might choose to step up with your pragmatic trust and begin to develop an emotional relationship with others, as you increasingly see them as deeply likeable and inherently trustworthy. You can then move one step further and see trust as a wholesome feeling founded on your shared values and vision. You begin to see the other as your confidant, a partner-in-crime (so to speak) and a person worthy of your deepest appreciation as a human. Certainly, you still need to rely on them in the pragmatic sense, but at the same time, you trust them in a way that goes beyond a business-like relationship into friendship.[**] Yet, to be able to develop any kind trust towards others, you need to begin by trusting yourself.

Trusting yourself and others

We trust leaders who trust themselves and who trust us. If you are mistrusting of yourself, you are likely to feel insecure, agonise over decisions, abandon those decisions at the first sign of difficulty, beat yourself up when things go wrong, and be reluctant to take credit for your success. On the other hand, if you are mistrusting of others, you might stick to bad decisions no matter what, and then blame others for the negative outcome while taking credit for any success.

---

[*]   I would dare to guess that pragmatic trust is the most prevalent form of trust in many organisations.

[**]   It is also possible to develop emotional trust without the pragmatic element. You can have friends you rely on privately but you may not necessarily want to engage with them professionally.

If you trust yourself and others, you will stand by your decisions, while remaining sensitive to the feedback from your team falsifying your assumptions. If you make a mistake, you will be able to acknowledge and take responsibility for it, without blaming others. It is because you know that mistakes happen, and you are able to move past them along with your team, without harm to either you or them. Finally, you will be skilled in accepting and sharing credit. Trusting and trustworthy leaders admit to their success, while shining the spotlight on their team. This is why it is a pleasure to follow them, and it is easy for the peers and superiors of such a leader to have trust in their abilities.

As easy as it may sound, trust is not something we usually have in abundance. It needs to be learned and practiced. Once established, trust tends to move to the background and become an invisible social practice that you and your team lives by.[*, 91] The bottom line is that trust and lack of thereof needn't be a taboo subject.[92] Too often, nobody dares express their mistrust and everybody keeps on pretending that everything is all right. If there is a reason for mistrusting someone, such a situation needs to be openly addressed and dealt with. Only then you can start rebuilding trust if it was somehow broken. It is an act of compassion in fact to help another person see how they might have acted in a way that was untrustworthy. You give them space to explain and alter their future behaviour, offering them a chance to regain the broken trust. The alternative is to keep on mistrusting, which only brings more mistrust as a consequence.

---

[*]   By the way, think of any moment when your organisation talked about 'empowerment' and everybody was sceptical. Why? Because empowerment too often means responsibility without trust expressed by autonomy and authority. No wonder nobody wants to be 'empowered' in this way.

You also need to quit the blame game, if it takes place. Mistakes are a natural part of any activity but if there is a prevalent assumption that everybody acted to their best abilities, there is no room for blaming and shaming. Both you and your team members aren't children to be scorned; you are all adults who understand their actions and their consequences. If your team members feel treated like valued adults, they will see you and each other as deeply humane, not as cogs in the machine. Such trusting appreciation is crucial because it leads to honest information sharing, tolerance towards others, effective collaboration and joyful interdependence — the ingredients for a great team culture.[93]

WEEK

VII

CHALLENGE

In order to build trust, it is important to first see the extent to which you trust yourself. It is also crucial to recognise why it is worth trusting those around you. One of the elements of such understanding is to see others not only as subject matter experts but as wholesome humans with a set of hard and soft skills that are crucial ingredients of your desired team culture.

YOUR EXPERIMENT:
Describe it in three sentences

Your deadline ....

Positive observations   Negative observations

√ ✕

Positive reactions   ☺ ☹   Negative reactions

Your conclusion ....

What to improve further? ....

CORE TASKS

1. Soft skills describe our personal competences such as social aptitude, communication capabilities, the ability to work in a team and other personality traits that characterise relationships between people. Soft skills are traditionally considered complementary to hard skills, which are our ability to skilfully perform a certain professional activity.

   Check out the list of soft skills. Choose those that you consider important for your team culture. On a scale from 0 to 3, assess how advanced each of your team members is with respect to the skills you chose. Then ask them to self-assess and discuss any potential discrepancies. How can you help yourself and them develop these skills?

An assorted list of soft skills [94]

☐ Adaptability to changing requirements
☐ Agility in the face of unexpected obstacles
☐ Authenticity and consistent behaviour
☐ Bouncing back from failure
☐ Coach-ability and the desire to coach others
☐ Collaborative mindset
☐ Conscientiousness in keeping promises
☐ Eagerness to learn from criticism
☐ Ethics even when not under scrutiny
☐ Ability to mange difficult conversations
☐ Motivation to take on new challenges
☐ Positivity towards forward motion
☐ Crisis management skills
☐ Decision making with effectiveness
☐ Delegation for productivity
☐ Diligence and attention to detail
☐ Entrepreneurial thinking and guts
☐ Facilitation of discussion
☐ Innovative problem-solving
☐ Conflict resolution instincts
☐ Ability to deal with difficult people
☐ Diplomacy in difficult situations
☐ Intercultural competence
☐ Assertiveness on behalf of ideas that matter
☐ Body language (reading and delivering)
☐ Charisma and the skill to influence others
☐ Clarity in language and vision
☐ Giving feedback without ego
☐ Leadership skills
☐ Negotiation skills
☐ Networking

☐ Compassion
☐ Endurance
☐ Enthusiasm
☐ Flexibility
☐ Friendliness
☐ Honesty
☐ Living in balance
☐ Passion
☐ Purpose-orientation
☐ Quick-wittedness
☐ Resilience
☐ Risk-taking
☐ Self-awareness
☐ Self-confidence
☐ Sense of humour
☐ Strategic thinking
☐ Stress management
☐ Goal-setting skills
☐ Lateral thinking
☐ Listening
☐ Prioritising
☐ Problem solving
☐ Troubleshooting
☐ Artistic sense
☐ Creativity
☐ Critical thinking
☐ Persuasion
☐ Public speaking
☐ Reframing
☐ Selling
☐ Storytelling

2. What does it mean to you to trust? Write ten points that describe how you are currently showing trust to your team. Which of these is the most difficult for you?

....

....

....

....

....

3. Using a scale from -10 to +10, assess how much you trust yourself as a leader. Now, list your team members, your peers and your managers, and consider how much they might trust you. What, do you think, is their trust or mistrust based on? Is it professional (eg, your financial director thinking that you are not optimally spending money) or personal (eg, someone is doubting your skills)? What can you change about your behaviour and way of being in order to build more trust?

4. Using the same scale (from -10 to +10), assess how much you trust each of your team members. If you find there are certain team members you don't trust, ask yourself why this is the case. What needs to change for you to trust them? Should they change? Or perhaps you? Now, take a look at those you trust. Is it pragmatic or emotional trust? What can you do to build more trust into your relationships with them?

EXTRAS

1. Vulnerability is one of the key skills necessary for building trust with your team. You can respect others for who they are and be honest about what they do. You can praise their actions or express disappointment when they don't act up to their ability without making it personal either for them or for yourself. On the scale from 1 to 10, how vulnerable are you towards your team? How vulnerable are they towards you? What can you do to create space for more vulnerability? How can you build a support system for yourself and your team members to be safely vulnerable?

2. Observe the emotional language within your team. Are your team members showing self-awareness, emotional control, self-motivation, and compassion? What works? What doesn't?

3. Do something that expresses your trust in yourself. Make it personal rather than professional. Perhaps you go for a go-cart race or to sing karaoke. Trust that you are able to do that.

LOOKING BACK

Trust, vulnerability and compassion are difficult topics to reflect on. They require you to look deep into your own convictions and insecurities. What did you discover about yourself this week? How did it make you feel? What is the one thing you might want to focus on as you continue? What can you praise yourself for?

Now, look more specifically back at the previous week:

1. How many core tasks did you manage to complete? How did they help you? Where were you stuck?

2. Did you run your experiment this week? What was it? What was the outcome? Was it noticed by others around you? Is it something you plan to continue with? Or perhaps you have another idea of how to alter and improve on it?

3. Is there space for Rule no 6 when thinking about trust? How could it work for you?

4. Was there anything else that resonated with you? What was it? Why do you think it was important? How does it help you define your unique leadership practice?

Daring To Dare

The dangers of 'know it all' attitude

The joy of being wrong

Dancing with your ego

Experiment!

Staying curious

This week's challenge

It was 1932 — the middle of the Great Depression in the US. The governor of New York, F. D. Roosevelt said, "It is common sense to take a method and try it: if it fails, admit it frankly and try another. But above all, try something". Experimentation (because it is what Roosevelt was talking about) is a crucial part of innovation. While many organisations embrace the idea of innovation, they seem less keen to consider that you can't have innovation without experiments. Creating an experimentation mindset is a big shift in attitude — moving away from thinking that 'only perfection is allowed and we must get it right the first time we try' to a mindset of 'I don't know, but I will find out.'

There is a prevalent misconception that innovation is about having ideas. Once you have them, innovation will magically happen. Certainly, coming up with ideas is a part of a process leading to possible innovation but it is not the most challenging part of it. The Business Dictionary defines innovation as, "The process of translating an idea or invention into a good or a service that creates value." Note that this definition focuses on the process and its outcome, not on the idea. Making an idea into a valuable result has hundreds if not thousands of variables that you are not able to see beforehand or argue around the table. Experimentation is fundamental to obtain new knowledge that leads to better decisions and greater solutions. So, if innovation is an idea that is successfully applied to the world, experimentation is the most reasonable way to verify chances for that success. It is a journey of sorts that starts with not knowing.

The dangers of 'know it all' attitude

We tend to think that we know a lot more than we actually do.* Such a conviction might make sense when the situation we find ourselves in is stable and predictable, alas, today's world is nothing like that. Surely, there is a certain amount of knowledge we have that we can rely on. However, it is increasingly important to realise what we don't know — as an anonymous author put it, "It ain't what you don't know that gets you into trouble.

---

* Such a 'know it all' attitude is known as an 'illusion of explanatory depth'. It is a belief that causes us to overlook gaps in our knowledge that can be detrimental to what we are trying to achieve. It may mean that you don't have sufficient knowledge about your customers or stakeholders, and it also may mean that you don't understand the capabilities and the hindrances of your own organisation.

It's what you know for sure that just ain't so".* Yet too often, instead of accepting the uncertainty of not knowing, we prefer to hold on to what we think we know. This feels efficient but in fact it's just a little lazy. What's even worse, we tend to apply a bias, known as *motivated reasoning,* in which our unconscious motivations, desires and fears shape the way we interpret available information. We see some pieces of information as our allies and we defend them, and others we consider our enemies and we either neglect them or straight up shoot them down.

The desire to know and to be right leads us to assuming one of three types of mindsets: the preacher, the prosecutor or the politician.[96] As preachers, we want everybody else to believe our opinions. As prosecutors, we set out to prove everybody else wrong. As politicians, we believe that we have the perfect recipe for what everybody else should be doing. We just need to 'win the elections' so that we have enough power to turn our ideas into reality. In all of these cases, we are so convinced about knowing that we close ourselves off from even considering the alternative (of not knowing).

As a consequence, we fall prey to two types of bias — the confirmation and the desirability bias. The confirmation bias leads us to see the things we *expect* to see and the desirability bias makes us see what we *want* to see. In both cases, we remain blind to anything that contradicts what we know. We don't see what we don't expect to see. We keep on not knowing what we don't know. Only after we allow ourselves to accept the notion that we know less than we think we know, can we begin to shift to a mindset of *cognitive flexibility.*

The joy of being wrong

Cognitive flexibility is a skill that enables you to switch between different concepts, and to adapt your behaviour to achieve goals in a changing environment. It helps you to see what works and what doesn't in reality,

---

*   According to the *Quote Investigator* this statement has been attributed to several prominent humorists over the decades including: Mark Twain, Josh Billings (pseudonym of Henry Wheeler Shaw), Artemus Ward (pseudonym of Charles Farrar Browne), Kin Hubbard (pen name of Frank McKinney Hubbard), and Will Rogers. Yet, it is unlikely that any of them is the actual author of this quote. Its creator remains anonymous based on current evidence.[95]

and stay flexible in your approach. It also helps you to simultaneously apply concepts from one context to another, critically evaluate current strategies and generate new solutions. In other words, it is the ability to learn about how to learn, otherwise called the 'scientist mindset'.[97] This is why, for example, superforecasters love to be wrong.[98] It is because they are terrified of being wrong in the long run. Thus, they are happy to be wrong in the short term. It means that they learn and therefore form a more informed judgement. They understand that being right involves stumbling, backtracking and rerouting. The scientists apply the very same attitude to their work (as expressed by Daniel Kahneman in a conversation with Adam Grant, "Being wrong is the only way I feel sure I've learned something").[99]

Scientists search for knowledge as it can be captured in a given moment, but they also understand that the future may render their conclusions wrong or irrelevant. They derive hypotheses, drive experiments and draw conclusions that are seen as new knowledge, not as the ultimate truth. The only ultimate truth is reality itself; all we are playing with are models or theories that try to describe the truth and while some models are (amazingly) good, some are bad and others are just dead wrong. To recognise and accept this requires confident humility, the ability to doubt your own assumptions, and the curiosity to discover contradictory arguments and perspectives. The physicist Richard Feynman beautifully described such a mindset in a series of lectures, *The Meaning of it All,* by saying:

> "The scientist tries to find more exceptions and to determine the characteristics of these exceptions, a process that is continually exciting as it develops. He does not try to avoid showing that the rules are wrong: there is progress and excitement in the exact opposite. He tries to prove himself wrong as quickly as possible".[100]

Yet, so many of us are not looking to "prove ourselves wrong as quickly as possible". Quite the opposite — we try to prove ourselves right rather than wrong. We skilfully and subconsciously avoid falsifying our preconceptions and assumptions, and seek proof that whatever we think and do is correct. This is, of course, gratifying. When others see what we see, we feel like experts. But at the same time, we most likely miss lessons that might expand our worldview, make us think harder and perhaps come up with new approaches and ways to act.*

Dancing with your ego

Our reluctance to admit our ignorance stems from our ego, the little dictator that resides in our heads reinforcing the feeling of self-importance, and controlling the interpretation of information that we gather from the world. You might have heard that ego is generally bad for leaders. I don't think it's that simple. Ego helps you have faith in yourself, dare to try things that you've never tried before and makes you seek the goals that feel beyond your reach (like writing a book about leadership).

However, when uncontrolled, ego can become the sheer destructive force that leads you into politicking, prosecuting and preaching. Overblown ego won't allow you to admit that you don't know something, won't let you change your opinion or see that you might perhaps need to work on improving things. It will make you see the fault in others and the virtue in yourself, rather than realistically assessing a given situation. Uncontrolled ego will do whatever possible to protect your self-image and feed you perspectives that reinforce your way of thinking. You may recognise your ego at work when the answer to the question, 'What argument would make me change my mind?' is 'Nothing'.

As a leader, you need to understand how your ego helps you and how it hinders you. It may not be the most pleasant exercise but the worst thing is to pretend ego doesn't exist. It will make you blind to its impact and therefore ego will start ruling you rather than the other way around. It will keep you attached to your ideas and prevent you from realising when your opinions are off the mark.** In the words of Richard Feynman, "you must not fool yourself — you are the easiest person to fool".[101]

---

*   Think about what would happen if you chose to approach your next experiment as an exercise in falsification rather than confirmation? How would you change the way you prepare it? How would you alter the way you observe what happens? Would you reflect differently on the results? Would it take you on a different path? Would it be more rewarding?

**   You might even need someone in your team to alert you as you might not notice it yourself.

Once you see your ego clearly you will have no problem realising that, most of the time, you are not the most knowledgeable person in the room on the topics relevant to the situation. This realisation helps you stay collaborative and to apply the mindset of a scientist who is more interested in learning than in being proven right. Consequently, you will start to see yourself as a contributor, rather than an oracle, and this will ultimately ease the pressure so many leaders put themselves under, allowing you to move from a sense of self-importance to a sense of teamwork.

Experiment!

Some years ago, I conducted an analysis of all the market-facing projects one of my clients made over a year. We wanted to see how many of their projects were advancing the perception of the company as customer-centric, which were neutral towards it and how many were detrimental. The hope was that at least 50% of the projects were perceived as having positive impact on their customers. The reality was much harsher. It turned out was that only 20% of all solutions released that year were praised by customers, 50% of solutions were seen as neutral and 30% were seen as clearly not customer-centric. We wondered why this was and concluded that once a given project was accepted by the management board and a business plan was drawn up, there was no way to alter or to stop it. And since a lot of resources and effort were put into making such projects happen, the danger of sunk costs rarely allowed the company to assess the outcome realistically, so a vast majority of projects were claimed to be a success (without much evidence from the market to back this up).*

When you see a project as a final design you have an, often false, perception that you know the best possible solution and you assume you know how to make it happen. You believe that, once all the steps are taken, that success is imminent. So, you look for the evidence confirming your beliefs and often avoid or neglect any counterarguments. You put your ego at the forefront and you preach, prosecute and politic

---

* What I would like to add here is that the problem was not only the leaders promising outcomes they were uncertain about. The main problem was the executives accepting these promises and assessing the quality of a given leader by whether they delivered on their promise rather than to see every project as an experiment.

to convince your superiors and your team how to proceed. You promise success, so there is no way that the final solution won't be such.

On the other hand, seeing a project as an experiment means that the 'promise' is stated in terms of a hypothesis rather than a concrete outcome. That is to say, you assume that once you do this or that, a given result might be expected. It also means you know what needs to happen before you make the decision to continue and what will cause you to stop or change the direction of the project. And becasue of this, you don't become attached to any given output.

What do you need to consider in order to see what you do as an experiment? First, it is important to check whether you are attacking a real problem that is of any significance. Then, you need to have it grounded in reality. So many actions are taken without a proper understanding of what's going on, and too often this is the reason they fail. By checking the extent to which reality matches your assumptions you might find out that you detected the right problem, or that there is an underlying problem that needs to be addressed first before you tackle the one you set out to resolve.

Once you are sure what dent in reality you would like to make, you need a hypothesis, criteria of success and a deadline. So many of us find ourselves in a web of ongoing experiments that never end. As an experiment is a learning process, it needs an end date (and sooner rather than later), otherwise how will you know when to analyse and integrate the learnings? If the result of the experiment confirms your hypothesis, great; if it disproves it, that's equally good. In fact falsifying your assumptions often provides faster learning than successes, as we tend to ask 'Why did it fail?' more often than 'Why did we succeed?'

As you reflect on an experiment you run, check with yourself how your reactions are changing. Often, when we define experiments in terms of success or failure, we feel tension. This feeling changes as soon as we remind ourselves that we are running that very experiment to challenge our assumptions. Why? It is simply because that there is no failure in falsification. In the worst-case scenario, you will prove yourself right. There is no fear, no shame, no losing face. The only failure here happens if you don't experiment at all, you don't set a hypothesis at the beginning, you abandon your experiment without drawing conclusions, or you don't learn from what happened.

So, perhaps, instead of repeating the Silicon Valley motto 'fail fast, fail often' we should start saying *learn fast, learn often* (in order not to fail)? Because at the end of the day, what you want is to intelligently iterate your ideas to improve them, rather than throw your efforts away. When you aim to learn, you stay curious as to what it is that you want to learn in the first place rather than doing random things in the hope that by the law of probability something will work out.

Staying curious

Curiosity is innate to humans.[102] It is an integral part of our brain wiring and a propulsive force that pushes us to act.[103] As Aristotle wrote, "It is our human passion to know, to seek novelty and to actively explore our environment to discover new things."[104] However, curiosity can easily be damaged by how we talk about it. If you tell a child that they are naturally skilled, you might discourage them from trying to get better at it. On the other hand, if you tell them that they worked hard to become good at something, you create a connection in their minds that hard work and exploration pay off.[105]

Similarly, you might consider how you are praising your team. Such praise should include recognition of the effort, rather than talent alone. Actually, you might consider the opposite — appreciating whenever your team members admit to their ignorance and see it as a driving force for curiosity and therefore growth.

But, in order to do this, your team need to feel safe. Psychological safety is the basis on which your team can experiment, rather than feeling they have to keep proving their point. If anyone on your team senses that you are trying to blame them for something, you become their sabre-toothed tiger.* Creating a safety net is, in other words, a way of providing safety for yourself and others to try out new things without the fear of being shamed for it. It basically means that you know you are not going to be punished if

---

* Animals use curiosity to monitor their environment, so that their nests are not endangered by predators. In such situations, curiosity is the difference between life and death. It draws animals out of their comfort zone to acquire knowledge. It pushes them to explore and learn. One of the best things about curiosity, as Aristotle pointed out, is the recognition of ignorance. It is impossible to be curious if you assume you know everything, right?

you happen to make a mistake.[106] It allows for speaking your mind and sticking your neck out without fear of having it cut off.

The important thing to realise here is that whenever we feel threatened (and it doesn't matter if it is an unkind word, unpleasant behaviour or a truly threatening situation), our brains see it as a life-or-death threat and trigger fight-freeze-or-flight response. In such a situation, we are likely to stick to our comfort zone, as doing so increases our chances that no mistakes will be made. Comfort zone is nothing more than the place where you continue to do the same things that you do now, with the same outcomes, which is the unwanted recipe for holding on to the status quo. Conversely, when we feel psychologically safe, we become more curious, open-minded, and persistent.[107]

Google's two-year study of high performing teams discovered that if the workplace feels challenging but not threatening, teams can sustain the broaden-and-build mode.* Julia Rozovsky, the analyst responsible for this study said,

> "Turns out, we're all reluctant to engage in behaviours that could negatively influence how others perceive our competence, awareness, and positivity. Although this kind of self-protection is a natural strategy in the workplace, it is detrimental to effective teamwork. On the flip side, the safer team members feel with one another, the more likely they are to admit mistakes, to partner, and to take on new roles. And it affects pretty much every important dimension we look at for employees. Individuals on teams with higher psychological safety are less likely to leave Google, they're more likely to harness the power of diverse ideas from their teammates, they bring in more revenue, and they're rated as effective twice as often by executives."[108]

Thus, if you want yourself and your team to thrive and energetically adapt to change, you need to feel safe and make everyone else feel safe too. Having a safety net stimulates the cognitive processes underlaying innovative thinking such as creativity, bravery and solution-finding.

---

*   The broaden-and-build theory comes from the field of positive psychology. It suggests that positive emotions we experience broaden our awareness and encourage novel, exploratory thoughts and actions.

WEEK

VIII

CHALLENGE

Experimentation is hard, there is no denying it. It demands that you, as a leader, make a radical shift from the *modus operandi* based on knowing things. Such a shift begins by understanding what mindset you are using and then creating a safety net for yourself and others that allows everybody to stay curious, innovative and able to question the status quo.

YOUR EXPERIMENT:
Describe it in three sentences

Your deadline ....

Positive observations   Negative observations

✓ ✗

Positive reactions   ☺ ☹   Negative reactions

Your conclusion ....

What to improve further? ....

CORE TASKS

1. Everyone of us falls into the modes of preacher, prosecutor and politician every now and then. Try to observe yourself for a week, and spot such moments. What triggers such postures in you? How does it relate to your ego?

   My triggers for preaching are: ....
   ....
   ....
   ....
   ....

   My triggers for prosecuting are: ....
   ....
   ....
   ....
   ....

   My triggers for politicking are: ....
   ....
   ....
   ....
   ....

2. We hate losing more than we appreciate winning. A perceived loss triggers in us a need to reestablish fairness through criticism, competition, or disengagement. One way to increase psychological safety is to approach conflict as a collaborator, not an adversary. Come up with five different ways of how you can do this. Remember that one of these ways can be applying Rule No 6.

   1. ....
   2. ....
   3. ....
   4. ....
   5. ....

3. Laura Delizonna, the author of *Mindful Leaders*, said, "If you believe you already know what the other person is thinking, then you're not ready to have a conversation."[109] As an alternative, you might try to avoid assuming that you have all the facts. You could, for example, state the problematic behaviour as an observation: 'It seems like your engagement recently dropped and progress appears to be slowing on your project.' Another way to provide a safety net is to invite the other person into a joint exploration of the reasons behind a problem you have observed. You could also ask how they would solve a given problem, rather than proposing solutions yourself. You could also offer assistance by asking, 'How could I support you?'

    Think of three different ways in which you could change your wording so that your team members feel safe in the face of a problem.

    1. ....
    2. ....
    3. ....

4. Think of how you can create an environment for experimentation. Consider the following:

    •   Do you tend to choose the first solution that comes to mind rather than seeking the best possible solution by sitting with the problem? What would be the way to give yourself more time to understand the problem before jumping to solutions?

    •   Are you taking hypotheses-based actions and measure their outcome and impact? If yes, how do you do it (describe your process to yourself)? How could you further improve it? If not, what would be the first step to start running experiments?

    •   What does it mean for your team that it is safe to fail?

EXTRAS

1. Seth Godin lists a number of symptoms indicating that you might be defending the status quo.[110] Mark the statements that resemble those you might have used in the past.
   - ☐ That will never work.
   - ☐ The labor laws make it difficult for us to do a lot of the suggestions [you] put out. And we do live in a lawsuit-oriented society.
   - ☐ Do you have some research showing that this will work?
   - ☐ If you had some real-world experience, you would understand...
   - ☐ I don't think our customers will go for that, and without them we'd never be able to afford to try this.
   - ☐ It's fantastic, but the salesforce won't like it.
   - ☐ The salesforce is willing to try it, but [a major retailer] won't stock it.
   - ☐ There are government regulations and this won't be permitted.
   - ☐ This might work for others, but I think we'll stick with what we've got.
   - ☐ We will let someone else prove it works... it won't take long to catch up.
   - ☐ Our team doesn't have the technical chops to do this.
   - ☐ Maybe in the next budget cycle.
   - ☐ We need to finish this initiative first.
   - ☐ It's been done before.
   - ☐ It's never been done before.
   - ☐ We will get back to you on this.
   - ☐ We are already doing it...
   - ☐ ...
   - ☐ ...

   What makes you say those words? How can you become more mindful next time you are tempted to use them to defend the status quo?

2. Draw your professional timeline from as early as you can. Mark all the perceived failures that happened along that timeline. Were they truly failures? What are the lessons that stem from these events? How did they impact your life today?

3. Once again look at the timeline you created. What happened before the events you consider as failures? What was the decision that led to these events? Is there a pattern? Could that be your imposter syndrome speaking? Or perhaps it is an irrational belief that led to them?

LOOKING BACK

April K. Mills, the author of *Everyone Is a Change Agent*, says, "It is not about driving people, it is about driving change".[111] Driving change instead of people requires helping your team get out of their comfort zones while maintaining their psychological safety. You need that safety too. What did you discover about yourself when thinking about it? How did it make you feel?

Now, look more specifically back at the previous week:

1. How many core tasks did you manage to complete? How did they help you? Where were you stuck?

2. Did you run your experiment this week? What was it? What was the outcome? Was it noticed by others around you? Is it something you plan to continue with? Or perhaps you have another idea of how to alter and improve on it?

3. How do you see experimentation changing your approach to challenges ahead?

4. Was there anything else that resonated with you? What was it? Why do you think it was important? How does it help you define your unique leadership practice?

Developing Infinite Relationships

The 'we' story

Words matter more than you imagine

Transparency and translucence

Clarity

Feedback

This week's challenge

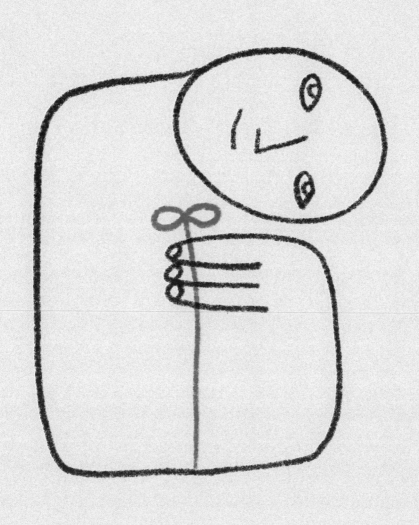

Whenever we interact with another person, we advance one of two kinds of relationships. In the first kind, we treat people as a means to an end, a tool that helps us obtain our goals. If we choose to pursue the second kind of relationship, we aim at creating long-lasting fellowships that help us engage with each other in a fulfilling and satisfactory ways while conjointly advancing our individual causes. Only this second approach to relationship-building enables creating a culture powered by compassion and trust rather than competitiveness and a zero-sum game.

The philosopher James Carse proposed that we form two kinds of relationships — finite and infinite ones.[112] If you approach a relationship as a finite one, you aim to 'win the transaction' and move on. An infinite relationship is a relationship that is intended to last. It offers you the space to show up as you — as someone with a potential to play, not with power based on what you've won. And if you think about it all fulfilling relationships are about playing rather than winning.

Carse compared building such infinite relationships to gardening. He said,

> "Gardeners celebrate variety, unlikeliness, spontaneity. They understand that the abundance of styles is in the interest of vitality. [...] Infinite players understand that the vigour of a culture has to do with the variety of its sources, the differences within itself. The unique and the surprising are not surpassed in some persons for the strength of others. The genius in you stimulates the genius in me."

Building such infinite relationships with others begins with creating a compelling story that becomes the basis of your team culture.

The 'we' story

If we look around, the narrative of 'us versus them' permeates political discussions, social issues, work conversations and even family relationships.[*, 113] Dividing our social world into inner and outer groups has its advantages, of course. Such mentality stems from the evolutionary need to belong to a group.[114] It further helps us to see who is a friend and who is a foe. But at the same time, it provokes us to associate

*   We tend to make a decision about whether someone belongs to our group or not within 170 thousandths of a second from the moment we see them.

with those who are similar to us over those who are different, preferentially allocate resources to and hold more positive beliefs about those who resemble ourselves. It also makes us exaggerate our status as well as go on the offence or defence to protect our territory. Sounds like a finite game, doesn't it?

What happens when we see the relationships with others as infinite rather than finite? Rosamund and Benjamin Zander write beautifully that,

> "It emerges in the way music emerges from individual notes when a phrase is played as one long line, in the way a landscape coalesces out of the multicoloured strokes of the Impressionist painting when you get some distance, and in a way a 'family' comes into being when a first child is born".[115]

They talk about interactions rather than arguments, about dialogue rather than opinions, commonalities rather than differences. This is the language of vitality creating a story of your joint *enoughness* and connection rather than insufficiency and disappointment. Taking this perspective is a choice all leaders face every day. Instead of asking, 'What are you going to do about it?', you have the opportunity to ask, 'How can we solve this?'.

The process of building the 'we' story starts with you, as a leader. You have the power to shape your relationships with others in ways that are genuine, while remembering that your team will be able to 'smell' your real intentions, much like bloodhounds. If you do this, they will intrinsically feel that you are in not for personal gain but with the infinite aim of integrating your team towards a common goal. So they will gather around you because they will want to become part of the story you are conjointly creating. It requires from you to blur the lines between people, to look for similarities rather than differences and to intentionally focus on the values and vision that you all share rather than on the elements that may potentially be divisive.

Words matter more than you imagine

All animals communicate, whether that be through chemical signals, colours, sounds or bodily expositions. As humans, we predominantly use words (along with gestures, intonation and body language, of course) as a way to share and exchange our various perspectives and to build our relationships with others. I would like to return to the concept of body budgeting from week 7 because the way we communicate has an enormous impact on this. As I mentioned previously, kind words calm us, while unpleasant or aggressive words aggravate our brains, flooding our bloodstream with high alert chemicals, causing stress and squandering our energetic resources.[*, 116] Scientists call this a *language network* that guides our heart rate, adjusts our glucose levels and changes the flow of hormones that support our immune system.[**]

I knew a company once, whose executives practiced a passive-aggressive communication style to badger their employees into acting according to their will. They demanded results, micromanaged and sometimes even shouted at those who didn't deliver according to their expectations. Interestingly enough, these same executives were shocked to learn that many of their employees thought of the organisational culture as toxic and harmful, and considered their employment there as only temporary. In other words, they were in it 'only for the pay'. These employees clearly saw that the executives were using them as a finite means to an end — the financial gain — which was directly reflected through their language and communication style because, in the end, any organisation is, to a large extent, a conversation.

Language you use is directly related to your organisational culture. It constitutes the ways in which everyone around you perceives their reality. It amplifies certain behaviours and types of relationships, while ignoring others. An organisational ability to create language is synonymous with its ability to evolve. It is because the language you use

*   It is worth repeating that our brains don't distinguish between different kinds of danger. It doesn't matter if you experience financial stress, relationship trouble or a mean boss, your brain sees it as a threat. If negative words are uttered in small doses (particularly if they refer more to your actions rather than you as a person), not much harm is done. But if you are exposed to them over and over again, without enough space and time to recover, the consequences are daunting. You will experience chronic stress, which over time literally kills your brain neurones and sickens your body.

** It is because many brain regions responsible for processing language are also responsible for controlling major organs and systems in our bodies, therefore any threat, be it physical or verbal, is seen as potential danger.

acts as a compass for your people, influencing how they think, act and feel in different situations. It doesn't mean that you need to tip-toe around everybody and exercise *cordial hypocrisy*. (Like I mentioned before, cordial hypocrisy is a tendency of people in organisations, because of loyalty or fear, to pretend that there is trust when there is none, being polite in the name of fake harmony particularly in situations that are conflict-prone). You just need to create space for nurturing conversations rather than harmful ones much like in personal relationships, for example, marriage.

In the 1970s, two American psychologists, John Gottman and Robert Levenson, run a decade-long study of romantic relationships.[117] The study begun with the couples resolving a conflict regarding the school they wanted to send their children to. Based on how they communicated, the researchers were able to predict with 90% accuracy whether they would stay together. It's not that the couples who stayed together didn't quarrel. The difference was found in how they balanced the number of positive and negative interactions during conflict. If one unkind word was spoken, they would compensate with five positive ones. They would laugh and tease each other as the discussion progressed, constantly expressing signs of affection towards each other. If, on the other hand, the positive-to-negative ratio in how a couple communicated during conflict was one-to-one or less, it was an indication that they were teetering on the edge of divorce. These couples kept on causing chronic stress in each other that would eventually lead to splitting up. It was, in a way, an escalation of negativity with no compensation.

We have the same needs in professional relationships. In any conflict, we seek some sort of compensation or simply appreciation for having the discussion in the first place. If we don't get this, we no longer feel part of the group and stop seeing a professional relationship as an infinite one. This is the moment when so many people start treating their jobs as a way to make money rather than to fulfil their professional aspirations, and sooner or later they prepare to 'divorce' that organisation. It means that they no longer see the organisation as 'theirs', and they emotionally separate from it. As my first boss, Roelof Hamberg, once told me, "If you are thinking about leaving your job, you've already emotionally left. Now, is it just a matter of time until you leave it physically."

Transparency and translucence

A nurturing conversation typically begins with understanding what is going on and what is being expected of everyone involved. In other words, you need transparency. Transparency is a great approach for stimulating infinite relationships and building an inclusive organisational culture. It involves explaining what is happening in such a way that others can easily see it too. Often, transparency is instigated by offering unlimited access to information, especially information about decisions and actions. It helps everyone to understand why others act in a certain way, to make reasonable plans and to coordinate action.[118] This is what makes our interactions socially sensitive and graceful.*

But transparency can also cause information overflow. Furthermore, some information may be too sensitive to be shared (for example, people's health issues or information about a deal that is not yet closed) and it should be hidden from sight of the rest of the organisation. Additionally, some people may not want full insight into many decisions, as not knowing allows them to think independently and stay creative while not being influenced by external sources of information.** This is why we may sometimes need translucence rather than transparency.

Two IBM researchers, Tom Erickson and Wendy Kellogg, described translucence with the following example:

> "In the building where we work there is a door that opens from the stairwell into the hall. This door has a design flaw: opened quickly, it will slam into anyone entering from the other side. In an attempt to remedy this situation, a sign was posted: *Open Door Slowly*. As you might guess, the sign is not very effective. We like to contrast the sign approach with a different sort of solution: putting a glass window in the door. The glass window approach is effective for three reasons. First, as humans, we are perceptually attuned to movement

---

* Too many organisations hide information such as salaries, which can easily cause gossip and therefore unnecessary disturbance and anxiety. This is why great human resource departments are so crucial—they have the necessary knowledge to balance out what should be transparent and what not.

** Ambiguity helps us see the non-obvious connections between things and discover new meanings.

and human faces and notice them more readily than we notice a sign. Second, once we become aware a person is present, our social rules come into play. I don't open the door quickly because I know you're on the other side and I've been raised in a culture that frowns upon slamming things into others. There is a third, subtler reason for the glass window's effectiveness. Even if I haven't been properly acculturated and don't care about harming you, I may still refrain from slamming into you because I know that you know that I know you're there, and therefore I will be held accountable for my actions".[119]

Translucence means that you share just enough of the significant information (rather than all of it).* Your job as a leader is make your team aware of why this specific piece of information is shared and what it indicates for your plans and actions.** In this way you ascertain that there is sufficient clarity in what you convey, while not having to discuss every detail. And in the case of both transparency and translucence, you need to make sure that everybody understands what you mean as well as have a way of providing feedback on the desired ways of acting based on the information provided. In other words, you need to implement accountability to make sure that everyone (including yourself) understands that they will be held responsible for their actions based on the information they have access to.

Clarity

Have you ever noticed how many people, when asked to explain their ideas, tend to repeat themselves (with an ever louder and more irritated tone of voice) rather than digging deeper into the reasons behind their proposals? Too often we think that we are clear about our motivations and plans, so we rush ahead and then wonder why others don't follow. Regardless of whether you use transparency or translucence as your communicative *modus operandi* you need to be clear about your motivations, expectations and intentions. Such clarity begins in your mind.

---

*   This means that you need to determine what is significant and what is not.

**   To be truly translucent, your job as a leader is to make sure that the informational bits are, indeed, something that your team expects, needs and is able to act upon.

You need to know what you want to share in the first place to make it clear for others. Then you need to make sure that what others heard was, indeed, what you had in mind.

There is a great example from the military tactics that can help you to make sure that others heard and understood what you had in mind, called *briefing and backbriefing.** It starts by sharing a given idea along with the 'why' behind it. The best way would be to link it to your vision but sometimes another explanation (like an immediate organisational need) might suffice. Then, you ask the team what they understood from your story and what it implies to each of them. If there is any misalignment you explain your ideas once more (in different words rather than with a louder voice) and make sure that this clarification is correctly understood.

It sounds easy enough, however, in many organisations, asking others to repeat what you said might feel, on the one hand, as if you are treating your team members like children, or, on the other hand, like the team is questioning your competence. This is why so many leaders shy away from it. They are afraid that they will be seen as controlling, or exposed as ignorant, or they worry they will be asked about things they can't talk about. This brings us back to the concept of translucence, which gives you, as leader, a way to explain to others what you can and can't share and to discuss whether the offered information is sufficient to act in an informed way. And if you worry about how your *briefing and backbriefing* landed with your team, just ask them for feedback about it. Such feedback will certainly help you to better prepare the information you intend to share with them in the future.

Feedback

Giving and receiving feedback is an essential part of the leader's job, and it starts by creating the right expectations (both for yourself and for the other person). You need to make sure that your feedback lands well, creates accountability and helps you develop your team. This can prove to be tricky though. Often, those giving and receiving feedback

---

* The habit of writing meeting minutes is very similar to *briefing and backbriefing*. It just misses the element of synchronously validating that everyone leaves with a similar understanding in mind.

are not on the same page as to the type of feedback they are sharing, hence there are so many feedback-related misunderstandings.

According to Douglas Stone and Sheila Heen, the authors of *Thanks for the Feedback,* when we receive feedback we want to either feel validated, or we want it to be an expression of a relationship we have with the other person.[120] What we don't want, however, is for our identity to be damaged by it. In that context, you can think of feedback as either praise, coaching or evaluation. Sometimes people just want to be appreciated for what they've done. This is a moment for saying 'thank you' without pointing out things that could be improved upon or aspects of the work that did not go exactly how you imagined. In other cases, someone wants to learn how they are doing. This is a moment for evaluation, for discussing where they are in their professional development, with its pros and cons. And there are moments where someone seeks coaching: tips and hints on how they can improve and become better at what they do. In a way, praise is about what happened in the past, evaluation is about what's going on in the present, and coaching is about the future. Thus, during the conversation you can always inquire whether the feedback you provide is what the other person looks for. This gives you an opportunity to clarify your intentions and also add the kind of feedback the other person was hoping for (if there was a mismatch of expectations).

So far I've been mainly talking about feedback from the leader to their team members but it is invaluable to create space where the team members share and receive feedback from each other (and, ideally, also from outside of your team) so the whole team can reflect on how to improve their ways of communicating and interacting.* Imagine it much like reflecting around the kitchen table, where together you discuss what you would change next time to improve your ways

---

*   A great example of such feedback practice is *agile retrospective*. It usually takes the form of a meeting held at the end of an iteration in agile software development. The retrospective can be thought of as a 'lessons learned' meeting where everybody on the team answers the following questions: What worked well for us? What did not work well for us? What actions can we take to improve our process going forward? Based on the collected insights, the team then decides what changes they want to make in the next iteration. The retrospective should be team-driven where team members decide together how the meeting will be run and how decisions will be made.

of communicating and acting. A major part of this process is offering appreciation. Since every single one of us wants to feel like we are becoming a better version of ourselves, we need to be assured this is, indeed, the case. Only then you and your team members will become open to any other type of feedback.

One last thing I would like to mention here is that feedback needs to be seen as supportive, not judgmental. April K. Mills calls this *practicing wound care.*[121] There might be different situations where some of your team members feel unjustly judged. This is why it is important to create space for healing those wounds, space where they can express what happened and how it damaged their trust in your organisation, or even in you as leader. In this way you further build a culture where psychological safety, vulnerability and trust are present. All these things make your team feel like they are in an infinite rather than a finite relationship with you and the organisation. It will make them more willing to take risks for an unknown future as they will believe that they are not alone.

WEEK

IX

CHALLENGE

Building a desired team culture that nurtures infinite relationships begins with understanding the language you use towards others and others use towards you. This week's challenge is for you to become aware of your communication style and also your feedback-offering practices and to analyse the language you use to share it.

YOUR EXPERIMENT:
Describe it in three sentences

Your deadline ....

Positive observations   Negative observations

✓ ✗

Positive reactions ☺ ☹ Negative reactions

Your conclusion ....

What to improve further? ....

CORE TASKS FOR THIS WEEK

1. Investigate your emotional language. Every day this week, try to reflect on your communication style when talking to your team, your peers and your bosses.

   - How do you deliver your message?
   - How do you express your emotions? (Do you express them at all?)
   - When you encounter a situation you didn't expect, how do you react?
   - If you were to describe your communication style how would you do so?

2. Considering in advance how your team might react to your message helps you ensure the content of your message will be truly heard. This is why it is invaluable to plan your actions by anticipating the reactions of others and your reactions to their reactions. When preparing for the next meeting, ask yourself:

   - What are my main points?
   - Which of these points is the most important to me?
   - What am I willing to give up?
   - What are three different ways my listeners are likely to respond?
   - What are the possible objections I am likely to encounter?
   - How would I respond to those counterarguments?
   - How else can I drive my points?
   - What is my mindset as I am entering this meeting?

Taking a third-party perspective will encourage you to rethink the language you use, reformulate your arguments and expose weak points in your position. It will also help you decide what is the outcome you are after and how you can design that discussion so everybody walks out happy.

3. Praise is one of the most powerful things a leader can offer their team. When well deserved and well delivered, praise gives others the drive to continue doing the caliber of work you want to see. This is no anecdote. Gallup found that giving praise has a profound impact on a company's bottom line.* Think of five things that your team members did that is praise-worthy. Create five different ways of praising them for it.

    1. ....
    2. ....
    3. ....
    4. ....
    5. ....

4. Asking for feedback on how you deliver your messages or provide feed-back to others will help you see blind spots in your communication skills.[123] Next time you provide feedback or deliver a difficult message, ask your team:

    · What worked and what didn't work about my delivery?
    · How did it feel to hear this message?
    · How could I have presented it more effectively?

    Consider what are the five things that you can change in your communication style to be better received.

    1. ....
    2. ....
    3. ....
    4. ....
    5. ....

*   Those answering *strongly agree* with the statement: "In the last seven days, I have received recognition or praise for doing good work" are responsible for a 10% to 20% difference in revenue and productivity. Also, employees who report that they're not adequately recognised at work are three times more likely to say they'll quit in the next year.[122]

EXTRAS

1. Look back over the past month. Assess once again how much time you spent on the following activities:

   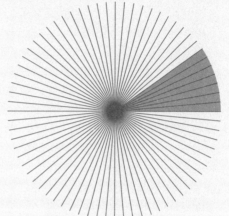

   · Working with strategy
   · Working with people
   · Working with content
   · Education of self and others
   · Enabling and coaching
   · Playing politics
   · Sitting in meetings
   · Evangelising
   · Recuperating
   · Other

   Do you see any changes compared to week 5? What are they? What do you tell you about the change you are instilling in your leadership practice? What are the things you need to focus on more? Are they difficult? If yes, then why? If not, what is stopping you from implementing them now?

2. Expressing your needs is an important aspect of communication. Think of ten things you would like to ask your boss for.

   1. ....   6. ....
   2. ....   7. ....
   3. ....   8. ....
   4. ....   9. ....
   5. ....   10. ....

   How can you frame them, so that they are well received? Think of the 'we story' as your tool. Select one of these needs and give it a try.

3. Analyse the difference between transparency and translucence. Take the next (or the most recent) piece of information you shared or are about to share with your team. What would be a transparent way to share it? What would be a translucent way? Where is the difference? How does it make you feel to share this particular piece of information in a transparent or a translucent way?

A transparent way is ....
....
....
A translucent way is ....
....
....

4. Regardless of whether you choose to be transparent or translucent with respect to the next piece of information you plan to share, the crucial aspect to remember about is to be clear about what you are conveying. Think of the next discussion with your team. How can you be clear about your message? Come up with five ways to express yourself clearly to them.

1. ....
2. ....
3. ....
4. ....
5. ....

LOOKING BACK

There are only three more weeks to go. Praise yourself for it because it's definitely praise-worthy. How did this last week go for you? How did your communication change? What are the things you are truly great at when it comes to interacting with others? What are the things you want to improve on?

Now, look more specifically back at the previous week:

1. How many core tasks did you manage to complete? How did they help you? Where were you stuck?

2. Did you run your experiment this week? What was it? What was the outcome? Was it noticed by others around you? Is it something you plan to continue with? Or perhaps you have another idea of how to alter and improve on it?

3. Did you offer praise to your team? If yes, how did it make you and them feel? Do you see any changes that can be linked with it? If not, what stops you?

4. Was there anything else that resonated with you? What was it? Why do you think it was important? How does it help you define your unique leadership practice?

WEEK

X

Making Decisions

A great deal of leaders agonise over making decisions.
Too many of these decisions feel like a huge responsibility
either because of their expected impact, or because they
are perceived as overwhelming as to what information
is relevant and what is not. This pressure stems from
the fact that we want to arrive at the perfect outcome.
What we don't realise is that there is no perfect outcome
as there is no perfect decision. All decisions are in fact
imperfect. Some are just less imperfect than others.
This can be a difficult notion to accept, particularly
in the Western culture. We are taught to think in black-
and-white terms about what we decide and how we act.
Yet, while making decisions, we operate within
shades of grey. And we often don't even recognise that
some of those decisions are not decisions at all.
They are merely choices.

What to have for breakfast? Which flight should I take? Which lunch would I like to attend? We make choices like these every day and sometimes we confuse them with decisions.*
A choice is about selecting between (usually not particularly significant) options that are equally good or equally bad (which also happens sometimes). A decision, on the other hand, is about strategically choosing the most promising course of action. You recognise a decision by its long-term consequences that are difficult to imagine at the moment of making it. Decision-making is a process that requires deep analysis to eliminate options, and it demands significant emotional labour.**
By contrast, a choice is an opportunity waiting to happen. You know it's a choice rather than a decision because, whatever you choose, the consequences most likely won't be significant or even long-lasting. So, if you find yourself agonising over a choice, make a rule to throw a coin, or select an option that comes first alphabetically.***, [124] It doesn't matter what selection scheme you have. Or, if you see little or no impact of a choice you are facing, don't make it and be at peace with that. Not choosing is a choice too, or rather, agreeing with whatever choice is made by others. In this way you will have more time and energy to focus on decisions.

---

* You can easily differentiate a choice from a decision by asking yourself—can I simply flip a coin to select my option? If the answer is yes, you are facing a choice.

** We've already looked into the notion of emotional labour in Week 2.

*** Imagine that you are choosing a restaurant for lunch—how about selecting the one starting with a letter A, B or C? Or imagine that you are wondering which shirt to put on before the next meeting with your stakeholders. How about choosing the third one from the right? It can really be that simple.

Before making a decision

Stop for a moment and think about a pressing decision you are currently facing. What feelings come up for you? The most frequent ones in such situations are: worry, anxiety, stress, nervousness, confusion, hesitance, discomfort or burden (and once in a while a little bit of excitement). These feelings are a sign of your discomfort when facing uncertainty. This is often the reason why we avoid making decisions, become overly hesitant or postpone them (sometimes forever).* We think that in this way we can handle the stress, while in the meantime, this very stress grows and quietly eats up our energy resources. We forget that our reasoning is never perfect and that, once in a while, we will make a suboptimal or even a bad decision, no matter how hard we try to avoid such a situation. Thus, instead of endlessly going round in circles about a decision, it is better to make one after a predefined (and limited) time and if it turns out not to be what you hoped for, admit to the mistake, take responsibility for it and correct it (if possible). Of course, it doesn't feel comfortable when you realise you could have decided better, but this is the only way to learn how to make more informed decisions in the future. In this way, instead of paralysing you, the decision-making process can become truly empowering.

What often stops us from admitting that we made a bad decision is our belief that that decision reflects badly on us, not on the situation. It hurts our ego to make a decision that turns out not to be what we have hoped for, particularly if it leads to negative consequences. I recall one situation in which my friend decided to lay off an employee, not realising that, as a consequence, a bunch of other people who respected this employee would also leave the company. When a situation like this happens, you need to give yourself the space to grieve very much like when you lose somebody or something important in your life. First, you feel shock that will turn into denial, then anger. You try to bargain, then experience deep sadness. Only after all that, you will be able to start looking for some realistic solutions to the situation at hand and, finally, arrive at a place where you may begin your recovery process.[125] Grief doesn't often come when the bad decision you took has moderate to little consequence.

---

*   These are also all signs of us not trusting ourselves as much as we should.

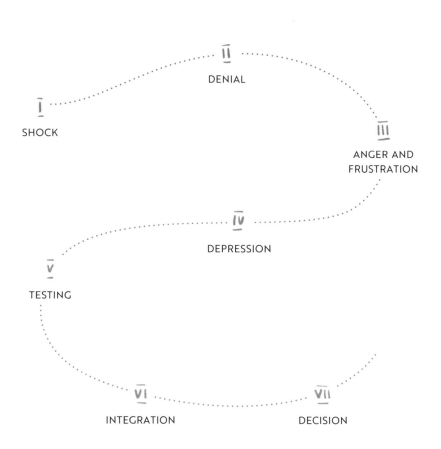

But, if its ramifications are significant and impactful of your's or some-body else's life you can be sure grief will most certainly turn up.

When it does, first, you need to accept the fact that it sucks to find yourself in a situation like this. Next, try to analyse what went wrong, and consider which of these elements were under your control, and which were beyond it. Now, consider where you can go from here, what are the options ahead of you that you can choose from to resolve the situation you found yourself in.* Once you have a range of alternatives, appraise them from the perspective of the future rather than the past. We tend to try to remedy what happened or to attempt to recover some of what we lost. But what happened happened, so now it is time to consider which course of action offers you the most promising future outcome.

When you analyse your bad decisions in this way, you will be able to see that each of them was made with limited data and therefore, by default, were sub-optimal with a dose of good and bad luck thrown in once in a while. Such a realisation will help you stay agile to identify when and how you can make better decisions in the future, with more or better information. Part of that agility is having the resilience to forgive yourself for a suboptimal decision that you made in the face of uncertainty.

The decision-making process

One of the core tasks of a leader is either making decisions or enabling others to make them. Decisions require you to envision the consequences of it being a good as well as a bad decision. You need to consider how easy it will be to recover from a bad decision and also what will happen if it goes well. Thus, the first step for you to make in the decision-making process is to articulate the decision you are facing. Why is it important? What about it matters? How will it affect the future? What consequences of making it can you see today? If you don't know the answers to these questions, you may not yet know if the decision you are considering is even the right one to make in the first place.

Another aspect to consider is whether making this particular decision is a priority task for you. You might have faced situations where what seemed urgent or important yesterday, is no longer urgent nor important today. Instead of trying to make that decision anyway, it is a good idea to make a new list of your priority decisions and focus on them. In this way, you will not be wasting energy on making decisions that you could hold off for some point in the future. This is important because, whether we are aware of it or not, we experience something called

*   Most likely none of them will be what you hope for—that is a sign of uncertainty at play.

decision fatigue. This means that our ability to make well informed decisions deteriorates the more decisions we make, as our brain gets 'tired'. Think of it as a finite source, like a battery. Each decision reduces the charge of the battery, and over time you have less energy available to make further decisions. *, 126 As a consequence, you may make decisions that are less well thought-through and more impulsive, increasing the risk of them becoming sub-optimal.

Something else to consider is that all decisions involve tradeoffs. As important as it is to consider what you can gain by choosing path B over path A, you also need to take into account what you might lose. Think of it as an opportunity cost — the cost of not gaining something because you chose something else. ** Imagine the following example. A small business owns a building in which it operates, and therefore pays no rent for the office space. This does not mean that the company's office space cost is zero. It is the opportunity cost. Perhaps the building could have been rented out to another company for profit, with the business itself relocated to another, less costly, location. Therefore, the foregone income from rental is not non-existent and should be seen as an expense.

Such an opportunity cost is not necessarily a bad thing. It is just the price we pay. Being aware of the notion of tradeoffs and opportunity cost will help you make decisions faster and be at peace with them and with yourself. Actually, not considering opportunity cost due to a long decision process is the biggest cause of lost value in corporations. You spend so much time making a given decision that you, for example, miss the chance to be first on the market with a new solution. As my mentor, Jørgen Bang Jenssen, kept on saying (after John Maynard Keynes), "It is better to be roughly right than precisely wrong."

---

*   There is an ongoing debate in the research community whether decision fatigue does indeed exist, partly due to the difficulty of proving its effects in any concrete way. Thus, it is still too early to make conclusive claims either way. Regardless of that, it has been shown in multiple studies that the decision-making ability decreases over time and with the amount of mental work exercised.

**   The *opportunity cost* is also known as *the cost of lost opportunity.*

So, in the process of making your next decision you might consider starting with the question my friend Rob van der Tillaart proposes — MUST I DO THIS TODAY? He sees this as a framework, where every word in the sentence has alternatives, and all must be consciously considered to initiate a decision-making process.

☐ MUST   ☐ SHOULD   ☐ COULD   ☐ WON'T

....

☐ I   ☐ MY TEAM   ☐ MY BOSS   ☐ MY PARTNER   ☐ MY SUPPLIER

....

☐ DO   ☐ DELEGATE

....

☐ THIS   ☐ SOMETHING ELSE

....

☐ TODAY   ☐ TOMORROW   ☐ NEXT WEEK   ☐ NEXT MONTH   ☐ NEVER

After the decision has been made

Your decision-making process may be longer or shorter, but one day, the decision is made. Whatever this decision might be, there will be consequences you didn't predict at the time of making it. What sometimes happens is that although a decision was well thought-through before being made, when unpredicted consequences arise, we have a tendency to either hold or revert our initial decision, rather than see it as a process of exploration-in-action. I've seen leaders deciding to approach a challenge in a new way only to quickly get back to doing things the same way they did before or as their competitors used to do as soon as they encountered the first significant obstacle. In that way, they tried to hold on to the feeling of control focused on minimising risk while losing sight on how to generate value through their initial way of thinking.

If you face such a situation, give yourself time to think before acting on your initial impulse because when encountering risky circumstances, your first impulse may be to minimise the exposure to the perceived downsides. In other words, it could happen that these downsides are preventing you from seeing the upside which may be waiting for you further down the road. Instead, in order to feel safer you may focus on identifying the foreseeable problems related to making a decision that you perceive as 'risky' not realising that it is your fear firing up wrapped up in the notion of regaining control over the situation.* But the truth is that, "You never had control, all you had was anxiety", as Elisabeth Gilbert, the author of *Big Magic*, once said on social media.[127]

If you find new insights that lead you to believe that there is a better course of action over the one you initially chose, don't hesitate to change your decision. Sticking with a bad decision is as bad as changing your mind too quickly. Imagine the following situation. You bought a concert ticket for $200. On the day of the concert you fall sick. If you go out, you will probably get even sicker. It seems like a reasonable thing to stay at home but the $200 investment will then go to waste. So, you drag yourself out of bed and against all reason you attend the concert (most likely not much enjoying the music and then falling even sicker). Such reasoning is known as the *sunk cost fallacy*. It means that we are likely to continue an endeavour if we have already invested money, time or effort into it. Thus, we go against evidence showing that the decision we made is no longer the best decision, costing us even more.

A famous business example of that fallacy is the story of building the Concorde. In 1956, the Supersonic Transport Aircraft Committee decided to build a supersonic airplane. The project was estimated to cost almost 100 million dollars, an investment made by French and British governments and engine manufacturers. At some point, it became clear that the costs would never offset the financial gains of the plane. Nonetheless, the investors decided to continue the project based on the fact that they had already put too much money and time into it. Ultimately, this led to millions of dollars being wasted, and the Concorde operated for fewer than thirty years with only twenty planes ever built, and just fourteen of them becoming commercial aircrafts. It happened because the investors could clearly see the costs involved but didn't quite comprehend that their initial investment, once made,

---

* We often focus on the concern or the risk that is most apparent, rather than delving into what may be at the root of that concern.

could never be recovered, regardless of whether the project was continued or abandoned.

As leaders, we need to train ourselves in 'killing our darlings' much in the same way as designers do. In the case of designers these are ideas, in the case of leaders — former decisions. Seth Godin once wrote, "New decisions based on new information are at the heart of leadership. But you can't make those decisions if you're also busy calculating how much the old decisions cost you."[128] Think of such decisions as a gift from your former self. You don't have to keep on using it if it doesn't serve you well any longer. The key here is to recognise that the quality of a decision-making process is separate and distinct from the quality of the outcome and the only thing you can do is to embrace the outcome, adapt and see it as a process of feeding your intuition.

Feeding intuition

For any decision that you make, you can define upfront a measure of success or failure. Thinking of these measures in advance can seem quite challenging, no doubt due to the lack of time. When your agenda is full and you are bombarded with information, giving space to thinking about success criteria feels next to impossible. However, if you don't know what success and failure might look like, how will you ever know whether the decision you made was good or bad?*

Setting your success and failure criteria doesn't have to be as hard as it may seem. You can define success as a stage that brings you closer to your goal (or at least not further away) and makes your team thrive (or at least doesn't hurt them).** You can ask yourself — 'Does this decision bring me closer to my vision?' Along with — 'Will my team be proud of delivering the outcome of my decision?' If the answers are positive,

---

*   Some organisations and their leaders fall into a trap of choosing their success criteria after the consequences of their decisions are already known. This might be a good defence in a politicised organisation but it prevents you from learning and feeding your intuition.

**   The time spent making that decision might be proportional to its importance. You could go so far as time-boxing the decision-making time. This may be quite effective, especially if you dedicate your full attention to making that very decision in the time you made for it.

it seems like your decision can be something to follow through with. Alternatively, you may consider possible failure by asking yourself — 'What could go wrong after this decision has been made?'* If the consequences are daunting, perhaps this is not be best decision to make. If you are really short of time, consider just one question — 'What will be the worst consequence of this decision (just one)?' Often, you might realise that that consequence is not too terrible, or even that there is no downside to a particular decision. But if you see a possible significant negative consequence, you will have a chance to adjust your decision or to change it before the negative consequences materialise.

Establishing success and failure criteria for your decision is an exercise in vain if you don't assess what happened after you took it. If you don't consciously consider what are the consequences your actions caused or influenced, your intuition will not get enough input to assess whether you should do things differently next time.

I acknowledge that analysing every decision is an impossible endeavour. However, there are a few decisions every day that carry a greater load than the rest of them. Revisiting them to see how they panned out could become an element of your reflective practice that helps you see the effects of your decisions and also becomes your learning tool for better decision making based on improving your intuitive thinking.**

---

*   You could use an exercise called *pre-mortem* to do so. This will help you understand what may not work, so that you can make corrections to your decisions before making them.

**   You may also use your council for debating some decisions and in this way, you will be able to see the possible consequences from the different perspectives of your council members. However, I realise that this is not a tactic for everyday decisions you face as a leader.

Prioritisation

Many leaders try to fool themselves into believing that they can make all the decisions that come their way. Barry Schwartz, the author of *The Paradox of Choice,* calls such a mindset a *maximising mindset.*[*, 129] There are two instantiations of that mindset when it comes to decision-making. We may try to make all decisions ourselves and we may agonise over decision that have many alternatives. Regardless of whether it's the first or the second case (or both), with the maximising mindset, we automatically fall victim to *the fear of missing out* (FOMO) because the only way that we can know if we made the best decision or we managed to make all possible decisions is to keep looking back, which ultimately reduces our satisfaction with the choices we ended up making.

The alternative is what Professor Schwartz dubbed as a *satisficing mindset.*[**] Satisficing is a decision-making process in which a person makes a decision that is satisfactory rather than perfect. When satisficers decide, they typically consider what they want to gain or preserve, and then evaluate their options taking into consideration what is good enough for them. And as soon as they find a choice that satisfies that, they go with it and don't look back. So, being a satisficer is about choosing what's good enough and also choosing based on what's known rather than worrying about what's unknown. This is, of course, easier said than done. You may feel that just being satisfied is not as appealing, that you need to maximise the outcome. But with the level of uncertainty,

---

[*]   A maximising mindset is rooted in a belief that more choice is better, even though having more choice makes us default to the old ways of thinking and acting. For example, if you have to choose among ten different options you are most likely to choose the one that feels most familiar. It is because the effort of comparing these options feels like too much, so the safest choice feels like the best way out. Also if you have tens or hundreds decisions to make you will be tempted to make decisions similar to the decisions you made in the past to reduce the mental effort of trying to figure out a new way of doing something.

[**]   The concept of the satisficing mindset was first proposed by the U.S. Nobel Prize-winning economist Herbert A. Simon, who created it by combining the words 'satisfying' and 'sufficing'. It is based on the assumption that It would require a great deal of effort — and may not even be possible — to gather all the necessary information in order to make the best decision, and satisficing thus represents the kinds of decisions we are actually capable of making.

leaders face on a daily basis, applying the satisficing mindset when it comes to making decisions will help you stay resilient and also daring whenever facing a daunting challenge of every leader — out of the impossible to complete list of decisions to make, which ones to focus on?

As inspiration, you may appreciate the story shared by Warren Buffett's pilot. Apparently, one day Buffett said to his pilot that he must have dreams bigger than flying Buffett around. After a moment of hesitance, the pilot agreed. Buffett then took him through three steps of prioritisation. Step one was for the pilot to write down twenty-five career goals. Step two was to do some soul-searching and select only five highest-priority goals. As step three, Buffett told the pilot to take a hard look at the remaining twenty goals. Those were the things to forget about as they were merely distractions that ate away his time and energy, and took his eyes from what was important. Buffett concluded that the pilot's five top-priority goals should get his undivided attention and be followed through with utmost investment.

I know that this story is about prioritising goals rather than making decisions; however, as you are starting your day, you probably have a relatively good idea of what decisions lie ahead of you. You could try to make a (limited) list with the decisions you need to make yourself and postpone the rest or delegate them to others. In this way you offer your team the opportunity to support you, and to shape the progress alongside you, which in turn builds trust and collaboration.

WEEK

CHALLENGE

Exercising decision-making is something not a single person can have enough of. This week, you will take a hard look at your decision-making process. Try to challenge yourself to tackle those aspects of making decisions that make you feel uncomfortable to see how you may improve your decision-making practices.

YOUR EXPERIMENT:
Describe it in three sentences

Your deadline ....

Positive observations

Negative observations

√ ✗

Positive reactions

☺ ☹

Negative reactions

Your conclusion ....

What to improve further? ....

CORE TASKS

1. Make a list of all the decisions you need to make this week. Which of them are actual decisions and which are choices? If you have to make a choice, choose the first option that comes to mind. That's it. How do you feel about it? Does it free up time for the decisions? How can you turn this into a daily practice?

2. Take one decision that you need to make this week and answer the following questions:

   • What is the outcome I want to achieve?

   • What are the options that I are choosing from?

   • What is the available information for each of these options and how do they intersect?

   Obviously, it will be impossible to apply the above exercise to every decision you face. Therefore, create a checklist (or a table) capturing the vision you defined in Week 4. Use it to consider whether the various decisions you are about to make are progressing or damaging it. How does this simple exercise impact your decision-making process? How much easier is it for you to make that decision after that analysis? When could you use such an analysis in your daily practice?

3. We are not trained to listen to our intuition, quite the opposite — often we are educated that we need to decide rationally. When facing the next difficult decision, go through your default process of deciding first. Then flip a coin. An exercise, such as a coin flip serves as a catalyst for finding out how you feel about the decision you just made. If you feel relief that the coin pointed at an alternative to your initial decision, rethink it, as apparently your intuition is telling you something different that your rational decision-making process. Whatever you decide at the end, you will gain an insight into what your intuition is telling you.*, [130]

---

* Flipping a coin is an academically proven aid for making decisions.

4. Learning from success and failure is crucial for training your intuition. Think of another decision that you are about to make and answer the following questions:

- What does success look like? Is it scary?
- What does failure look like? Is it scary?
- What do you need to succeed?
- What will you do if you fail?

EXTRAS

1. Professor Barry Schwartz talks about the maximising and the satisficing mindset. We often tend to apply the former over the latter when first making decisions and then considering their consequences. Take a decision that you recently made that you are not entirely happy about and list five consequences it led to. First, look at them with the maximising mindset and check why you are not entirely happy with the outcome. List what's missing. Next, put your satisficing hat on and consider what was the 'good enough' outcome of that decision. Do you see it with different eyes now?

2. There is one more aspect related to decision-making worthwhile considering. As you consider how you want to lead, you might find yourself afraid to take risks. Answer the following questions and observe what surfaces:

- What is daring leadership for you?
- How can you be daring?
- What are you afraid of as a decision-maker?
- Now, what are you really afraid of?
- Why are you afraid?
- How can you change your mindset?

LOOKING BACK

There are two more weeks left of this course. You are almost there! Take a moment to look back at the past two months and consider the biggest change you observe in yourself. How does it make you feel? What else changed? What are you more confident about? What still bothers you? What makes you feel proud?

Now, look more specifically back at the previous week:

1. How many core tasks did you manage to complete? How did they help you? Where were you stuck?

2. Did you run your experiment this week? Did you manage to run both of them? What were they? What was the outcome? Is it something you plan to continue with? Or perhaps you have another idea of how to alter and improve on it?

3. What are you most proud of as you are moving towards the completion of this course?

4. What are you more relaxed about in your daily work? Are you able to find more time for yourself? How does it work for you?

5. Was there anything else that resonated with you? What was it? Why do you think it was important? How does it help you define your unique leadership practice?

Becoming an Influencer

When I was at school, back in the pre-internet era,
we considered our teachers to be the gods of knowledge.
We were expected to absorb that knowledge, like thirsty
travellers drinking from a well, and then hold on to it
for the rest of our lives. Then, the internet came and that
information asymmetry disappeared in a puff of smoke.
Suddenly, we had unlimited access to any piece of data
and we could know as much as any other person on
Earth (including our teachers). Thus, if you were
able to figure out the question, you were likely to find
a set of answers to it without much assistance.
Those who used to guard knowledge (like teachers)
lost their unique position. Their help was needed only
when you either couldn't figure out what the problem
was or if you needed to convince others to buy into
your idea. So, instead of just knowing things, it became
important to be able to influence others to see a given
situation in a fresh light, to surface issues they didn't
realise they had, or to point out possibilities they
couldn't see for themselves.

S elling has a seriously bad reputation. When you think of the word 'selling', most likely your first image will be of a used-car sales-man from the 1990s — a greedy, pushy smooth-talker.* This is why whenever leaders hear that their job is to sell, they feel shivers going down their spine. Yet, you are selling ideas, approaches, news. You persuade, motivate, inspire, convince, influence — these are all selling techniques of great leaders. Influence is not about directly impacting another person's actions or behaviour by telling them to do something or by manipulating them. Instead, you notice what motivates your team and use that knowledge to leverage their engagement.

Daniel Pink shows that any person in the world spends about 40% of their waking time on something akin to sales. When you are a leader, this percentage goes up significantly.[131] If you map out your days, you will see that a large portion of your job is trying to influence and persuade others to do certain things, not to do other things, or do those things differently. This is selling, like it or not. Fortunately, this kind of selling is nothing like the job of the used car trader from the 1990s but resembles much more the influencers' movement, that begun around 2012.

Leaders who are influencers are those whose opinions are sought after and trusted. They are the thought leaders, mentors, and go-to colleagues. They are usually great networkers, helping people to connect to each other, often becoming the informal communication hubs across their organisations. They are usually known as effective problem solvers who operate in a gentle and inclusive manner. Leaders-influencers know how to make others look good. They are able to see themselves as contributors and supporters, and often score highly on compassion.

---

*   If this is not an association you are familiar with, you might like to check one of these three films: *Matilda, True Lies* or *Cadillac Man.* All three are great movies that will give you a picture of a typical 'salesman' from that era.

Influencers are able to convince those the most unconvinced about the ideas and decisions they themselves believe in. This is because they can clearly see that success is never theirs alone, it is always the result of teamwork. Influence happens when people 'buy into you' and the relationship they have with you. Building such a relationship requires you to zoom out from your own narrow perspective and self-interest, create win-win outcomes, be socially responsible to what is best for the team and the organisation, and focus on *how* you get the desired results. In other words, what you are after when trying to become a great influencer is a creation of genuine infinite relationships with those around you.

Connecting stories

Can you recall a situation when your boss told you to do something that you didn't agree with? Most likely your reaction was to resist that proposal. You grew a little frustrated and tried to exercise your own power to change that situation. You might have told them how this extra task affected your other assignments. You might have mentioned time pressure. You might have argued why your current project was more important than what they wanted you to do (probably even using arguments you heard from your boss). All of this likely failed as your boss exercised their power too and forced you to do what they wanted done. This is where their potential for influencing you went sideways.

Here's a surprising truth — if you want to sell well, if you want to increase your influence over another person, you need to *decrease* your power, not increase it. There is an inverse relationship between power and perspective taking, and for this you need to be able to take the perspective of your 'opponent' in order to understand where they are coming from. Such knowledge and attitude give you the tools to connect your story to their story.

"Every villain is a hero of their own story", wrote Christopher Vogler in *The Writer's Journey*.[132] Whenever analysing a difference of opinion, it is inevitable to conclude that nobody is irrational when it comes to holding a viewpoint. Yes, the joint rationale might seem incongruous but the individual perspectives make perfect sense. Let's take the situation we started with. Your boss has an idea and wants to push it forward and you disagree. Are you irrational? Far more likely, you see some sort of danger in what they are proposing. Or maybe you have an alternative idea and want it to become the preferred choice. Or you try to maintain your position as a threshold guardian of some cause your boss may not even be aware of. Whatever it is, if it doesn't get surfaced and addressed, your participation in your boss's endeavour will remain reluctant and disconnected. It is exactly the same with you and your team.

General Stanley McChrystal points out that in war conflicts a party rarely acts in an irrational manner.[133] They just act according to their own interest — be it victory, survival, protection or revenge. Understanding that interest helps to define a strategy that builds common ground, which consequently can lead to conflict resolution. However, finding that common ground requires us to detach ourselves (even if only temporarily) from our perspective; from our need to be 'the hero'. It requires us to let go of our own best interest and look for the joint best interest, of making someone who seems an enemy become a hero as well.

Creating common ground

When you and I engage in a conversation, neither of us is able to predict how we are going to react to each other's words and what course of action we are going to take as a consequence of that conversation.[134] This is why we need to keep checking at all times that we understand each other's reasoning in the same way. We also need to be able to find similarities, rather than focus on the differences in our reasoning. This is what common ground is all about. Common ground is a mindset that is based on a set of joint values from which the culture of a group is created and maintained. It is about creating opportunities to understand and integrate different perspectives — much like weaving a cloth out of individual threads of different hues.*

Common ground is built when every voice is embraced, and through the process of building common ground, the vision, priorities and ways of doing things become owned by everybody. For all to feel a sense of ownership in the common ground, everyone needs

---

* Sometimes there can be so much common ground that both people are literally thinking in the same ways.

to shift from sticking to their own part to focusing on the whole. There is shift away from individual agency to the ownership by the collective. You can tell that you have common ground when you feel comfortable and at ease during a conversation. There's no tension or anxiety, and you truly enjoy communicating.*

Building common ground begins by seeing each conversation as a deeply social act in which everyone wants to feel seen and respected.[135] For example, some of the people you will be convincing might fall into the category of 'early adopters' while others will be sitting firmly in the 'conservative' camp. The early adopters are easily excited by new ideas, so you might not have to generate a lot of arguments to get them to agree with you. They are often inspired by your ideas and 'innovate' on top of them. However, early adopters are often easily swayed by the next new idea that comes their way, so whatever you convinced them to do might be overwritten by the next person. They can also easily expect more than you can deliver, so it is important to manage their expectations. On the other hand, for the conservatives everything must be proven, and they prefer the idea to be tried and implemented somewhere else first. You might need to invest time and energy and perhaps find examples that prove to them that your idea is not as risky as it may seem. It may feel cumbersome, yet it is likely that once you convince the conservatives, you will have the necessary support in the future.

Of course, these are the extremes with the entire pallet of shades of grey between those two stances. Regardless of the posture a person you are trying to convince presents you need to start from where they are, not where you'd like them to be. Often, we sing about a bright new idea, not quite realising that we challenge another idea, which this other person might be contributing to or in some sense guarding. There is a chance they will become a little hostile, which may, in

---

*   Here's a problem though. Many of us try to establish common ground with the least effort, which, although it might seem efficient, causes unnecessary misunderstandings that need to be explained and corrected later on. This is why, regardless of the goal you have in mind, you need to make sure that you and your team buys in to what each of you is saying. In other words, you need to make sure that everyone understands your motives and sees them as justified. You want them to think that you are making a good point.

turn, provoke you to express some hostility as well. If this is the case, both of you start seeing the arguments as either attack or retreat. The inventor and the founder of Y Combinator Paul Graham's *Hierarchy of Disagreement* demonstrates seven levels of disagreeing with another person, starting with 'name-calling' and ending with 'refuting the central point'. All these tactics are in fact war tactics contradictory to building common ground. They focus on the substance of disagreement, pulling you and your opponent deeper and deeper down the rabbit hole of disagreement. Such tactics are the arguments typically used by preachers, politicians and prosecutors — the postures reinforcing personal 'blindness' that we looked into during Week 8.

. . . .

**REFUTING
THE CENTRAL POINT**
explicity refutes the
central point

. . . .

REFUTATION
finds the mistake and
explains why it's a mistake
using quotes

. . . .

COUNTERARGUMENT
contradicts and then backs it up with
reasoning and/or supporting evidence

. . . .

CONTRADICTION
states the opposing case with little
or no supporting evidence

. . . .

RESPONDING TO TONE
criticizes the tone of the conversation without addressing
the substance of the argument

. . . .

AD HOMINEM
attacks the characteristics of authority of the opponent
without addressing the substance of the argument

. . . .

NAME-CALLING
uses statements ad personam
sounding similar to, 'You are an ass hat.'

. . . .

So, rather than going for any one of these tactics, you may side-step by showing curiosity towards the other person and their argumentation. You can admit the points of convergence between your ideas, showing that they are not as far apart as they might have initially seemed. This is what turns attention your way and de-escalates emotions. It shows that you are willing to negotiate and to find a way that is satisfactory for everyone. In other words, you make everybody a hero of their story.

Once you have the attention of others, the next crucial thing is to make your proposal both purposeful and personal. Making it purposeful means showing how the world (their world) will be a better place once the idea is realised. Adding a personal element makes you relatable. (For example, you can build on a variety of subjects, such as a cuisine or a sport you all enjoy.) Quickly, you will find that you are conversing rather than defending your point. Having something in common builds your personal credibility and makes others believe that you will be at their side each step of the way. These common ground ingredients will likely make you be seen as reasonable, which literally means 'able to be reasoned with' — open to evolving your ideas in the light of new arguments and data.

The power of asking questions

It is a deeply evolutionary trait to act rather than to deliberate over options (which is the basis for creating common ground). When our ancestors saw something moving in the bushes, they didn't have the time to ask questions or consider alternatives as to what the possible danger might be. They had to act or be eaten. Although we are not facing such threats today, many discussions are an apt equivalent of that very scenario from the past. This is why we love to provide solutions, or at least offer advice. * Even if common ground is established, the other person is likely to have their own ideas on what needs to be done. Thus, your challenge is to help them see things your way, making them want to do the very thing you have in mind based on *their* arguments, not yours.

---

*   This desire to always seek solutions is further reinforced by our brains' need for clarity and certainty. No wonder we love to think in terms of answers.

Daniel Pink describes this as, "challenging people to do something that *they* want to do" rather than "challenging them to do something that *you* want them to do".[136] It is about making them dance to their own song rather than to yours.* The best way to achieve this is to ask questions. Questions are a way of helping others see what the preferred course of action is without explicitly telling them what it is. They are a way to suggest things, making them easier to accept. And, most importantly, questions let you learn from the answers of others that you hadn't considered yourself.[137]

Asking questions might feel like a rather ineffective strategy to get your point across. It is, however, quite the opposite. By allowing others to arrive at your arguments themselves, you make them not only more committed to the chosen direction, but also much more clear on what needs to be done. Moreover, the habit of asking questions helps you to become a better listener. It requires you to deeply listen rather than just wait to jump in and start sharing your perspective. It is important to remember, though, that questions work well when you are in the right and have logic on your side. How about situations when you are not entirely sure?

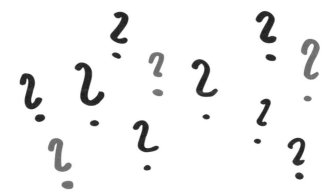

---

*   If you've ever attended a silent disco, you'll know exactly what I mean.

Thinking in alternatives

In his book *Why Decisions Fail,* Paul Nutt refers to a study he ran with over 400 executives, which showed that about 70% of decisions made in organisations are not treated as decisions but as binary choices: should we or should we not do it?[*, 138] So, it's not a surprise that about 50% of those decisions fail. The success rate increases dramatically when the executives are presented with more than just two alternatives to choose from. It is as simple as asking the question: 'What else could we do?' Such a question generates more possible courses of action and therefore increases the chance of a better decision by 30%.[139] This works so well because, as humans, we are skilled comparators. This skill is developed when as infants we try to figure out which of the people around us is our mother. The ability to make comparisons — to set one object or idea against another and take note of similarities and differences — is the basis of our learning. And since we are used to it from an early age, we make better judgments when presented with alternatives.[140]

Think of the following situation. You see one project proposal, which you are not happy about. It is the easiest thing in the world to say 'no' to it, isn't it? Now imagine that you have two proposals. You can see elements of each that you like and some that you don't. This already gives you new ideas about how the final proposal could be shaped. Now, imagine three proposals in front of you. None of them is great but now you can see even more of the different elements in each of them that excite you. This is typically a moment when new choices emerge, when parts of one proposal solve the weak points of another one enough to create something better. In this way you create a fourth proposal that is born out of the three; one that you and others are most likely to agree on and, even more importantly, commit to.

Here's another interesting aspect of providing alternatives. While two options are better than one and three options are better than two, four options are less effective than three. Having four options actually diminishes your persuasiveness as it seems like you are trying too hard. Offering four or more alternatives creates cognitive load,

---

*   Interestingly, this is similar to how teenagers decide.

overburdening our working memory with information and leaving people less likely to choose a new way of approaching the problem, and instead triggering what professor Barry Schwartz calls *the paradox of choice.* [141, 142]

The paradox of choice stipulates that while we might believe that having many options enables us to choose the one we are happy with, having an abundance of options requires more effort to make a decision and can leave us feeling unsatisfied with what we chose. It is because when the number of choices increases, so does the difficulty of knowing what is best.*

Multiple-step decisions

Even after you provided your stakeholders with the alternative proposals, it is important to realise that their decision process might be comprised out of several stages. In other words, your stakeholders will most likely need a number of steps to arrive at a final decision. Think about it this way. Buying a doughnut is a one-step decision. You want something sweet, you enter a bakery, look around and choose the thing that looks tastiest. Ordering in a restaurant is a two-step decision. You get the menu, look through it and then decide. Purchasing a car is a three-step decision (at least). You go to the car-trader to look around. Then you take the chosen machine for a test drive. Only then you might be willing to make a purchase.

Similarly in business, most decisions can be classified as one-, two-, three-, or more-step decisions. Yet, many people (particularly those with hot-headed personalities like mine) tend to see each of them as buying a doughnut. Sure, in our heads it is a simple decision. We have had all the time in the world to consider our proposal and see how great it is. But our interlocutors did not. They just heard about it for the first time. They may need time to consider it, maybe take it for a spin before they are ready to commit.

If we squeeze a many-step decision into one step for our stakeholders, the answer will most likely be 'no'. Saying 'no' is the easiest way

---

*   And we are back to the problem of the maximising mindset we looked into last week.

out of an uncomfortable situation or from feeling pressured. Creating the conditions to take more time for 'taming your idea' does not guarantee a positive outcome, but it certainly increases the chances for it.

So, if you want another person to make a decision, think how many steps they would need to take. If it is a decision that requires more than one step, consider how you can define those steps in the optimal way. Maybe the first step would be to check out what your stakeholders think about the general direction of your idea. Then you give them the time to think things over (even if for five minutes over a cup of tea, but preferably longer) and afterwards ask for their comments. Giving people time creates a feeling of them being in control.

The next step could be to show them your alternatives and ask for comments. Hearing out their opinions shows that you are interested in their perspective and willing to take it into account. It is a process of creating common ground when you try to find an outcome that is satisfactory (or at least acceptable) to everybody. Only in the last step might you want to ask for the final decision. It feels like a lot of unnecessary work and time but in fact you are creating for yourself favourable conditions that increase your chances for success.

What if your arguments fail?

Obviously, some of your ideas will be rejected. This is something we find deeply uncomfortable, as humans are not particularly good at dealing with rejection. It can feel that, if our idea wasn't bought by others, we personally failed. Many of us despair that rejection is a representation of our self-worth and that it is our fate to keep being rejected.[143] Yet, it is insane to see your self-worth through such a lens, isn't it?

I spent over ten years living and working in The Netherlands. There, I observed that the Dutch are able to cleanly disconnect their self-worth from the worth of a proposal they put forward. They understand that who they are and their ideas are two different things. More often than not, they know they are good at what they do but they also understand that sometimes even the best of us come up with an idea that is either not as good as it could be or that others might propose something more suitable to the situation. The Dutch then accept the outcome and learn from it, rather than despair.* They know that it is not going to ruin any-thing because they will soon come up with another proposal that will be accepted.**

If you feel uneasy about failure think about what you are comparing it to. Not getting your way? If you see rejection as independent of yourself (like the Dutch), it opens up a space for analysing what you could have done better, both about the proposal itself and also how you were selling it. Sometimes you will discover that you did everything right — you used your soft skills combined with convincing argumentation, you created common ground and provided sufficient time to consider your ideas and yet things beyond your control were the reason your ideas were rejected. The only thing then is to (as my favourite singer Diana Krall sings), "pull yourself up, dust yourself off and start all over again" knowing that it is not the end of the world and that you will have many other opportuni-ties to present your ideas and influence others to follow your lead.***

---

*   In Dutch, such an approach is known as 'polderen'.

**   What they dislike is if you do not speak out, and keep your wisdom for yourself. There are even courses to learn the Dutch way of thinking and speaking up.

***   *Pick Yourself Up* is a song composed in 1936 by Jerome Kern, with lyrics by Dorothy Fields, initially performed by Nat King Cole back in 1944.

WEEK

CHALLENGE

If you are as uneasy about selling and influencing as I am, you might be dreading this set of tasks. These tasks, however, are the way to ease that uneasiness and to find your own approach to getting your proposals accepted. Some of you might love asking questions, some of you (like me) might prefer working with alternatives. This is the time to find your preferred way and to see how you can rock it.

YOUR EXPERIMENT:
Describe it in three sentences

Your deadline ....

Positive observations   Negative observations

✓   ✗

Positive reactions   ☺   ☹   Negative reactions

Your conclusion ....

What to improve further? ....

CORE TASKS

1. As much as any rejection feels personal, permanent and pervasive, it rarely is. List five of your pitch failures.

   Your pitch failures:
   1. ....
   2. ....
   3. ....
   4. ....
   5. ....

   How hard is it to remember these failures now? Were any of them permanent, meaning did the consequences last until today? Did they ruin anything? Was it really personal? If you were to think about these failures now, what, do you think, were the reasons behind them?

2. Think back to your pitch successes now. List five of them.

   Your pitch successes:
   1. ....
   2. ....
   3. ....
   4. ....
   5. ....

   What were your best arguments? Why did they work? What do these successes say about you?

3. The most effective question to ask yourself before putting any proposal forward is: what's in it for them? If you are able to understand that you are half way to victory. List three of your most important stakeholders:
   1. ....
   2. ....
   3. ....

Write three things for each of them that they want or need:

· in general as people,
· as people in certain positions within your organisation,
· in relation to you and your team.

Think of your next proposal. What arguments can you build based on the needs of your stakeholders that are likely to convince them of your idea?

Argument 1 ....

Argument 2 ....

Argument 3 ....

Argument 4 ....

Argument 5 ....

EXTRAS

1. One way to get people on board with your ideas is to provoke them to imagine an ideal future and then work your way back to the idea you want to share with them. Instead of sharing your next idea straight away, ask your colleagues to envision the ideal solutions that would work in ten years. Then ask them to come up with five ideas of what the first step towards that ideal future would be. Throw your ideas in the mix and see what they think of them.

2. Think of the next proposal you are about to present to others. Come up with three alternative options: one that is conservative, one that is radical and the third one that is in the middle between these two. Show all three concepts and see the reactions. What changed compared to a situation when you had just one proposal?

   A conservative option ....

   ....

   An intermediate option ....

   ....

   A radical option ....

   ....

3. Go to a bakery and buy a doughnut to experience a one-step decision. Then go to a restaurant to experience a two-step decision of ordering a meal. Now, consider your team member coming to propose something to you. How many step decision should it be? How can you help others to start thinking in those terms?

LOOKING BACK

Selling is an emotionally difficult topic for many of us. It has a tendency to rub us the wrong way somehow. Take a moment to consider what emotions you are experiencing with respect to it and where they come from. How can you define selling for yourself so that it fits your world-view? What would make you become more confident about it?

Now, look more specifically back over the previous week:

1. How many core tasks did you manage to complete? How did they help you? Where were you stuck?

2. Did you run your little experiment this week? What was it? What was the outcome? Was it noticed by others around you? Is it something you plan to continue with? Or perhaps you have another idea of how to alter and improve on it?

3. What flavour of selling do you think suits you best? Why? What else could you be happy about?

4. What is your attitude to rejection? How can you convince yourself that it's not about you? How do you see your self-worth now? How can you pamper it?

5. Was there anything else that resonated with you? What was it? Why do you think it was important? How does it help you define your unique leadership practice?

Your Leadership Wabi-Sabi

Embracing tension

Building resilience

Embracing your leadership wabi-sabi

Change your ways and the world will reward you

This week's challenge

Today's world is one in which it is impossible to predict what will happen.* When living in such a world at the pace our lives take, it is inevitable that we experience stress. Such stress is further aggravated by the growing number of interactions in real or so-called 'social' networks, driving us toward constant availability and an expectation of having a near-instant opinion on any subject. Evolution did not prepare us for something like the industrial revolution, let alone the information streaming at us through the internet. We can cope with it, sort of, but still stress has become unavoidable. Yet, we hope for stress-free lives, not realising that not only is this impossible but that, without it, life would be less exciting and therefore possibly less worth living. Thus the goal is not to avoid stress but to dance with it to your own tune.

---

*   I am writing these words just as an unimaginable war is unfolding outside the border of my country—an unimaginable aggression of Russia on Ukraine. And I can see first-hand how deeply it affects everything that is happening every hour of every day: every decision, action, or inaction.

I f I were to ask you what stress is, you would probably mention everything you don't want to deal with: the chaos, the uncertainty, the crises, the conflicts. Experiencing stress as a leader might even make you wonder whether you are up to the job or you should find a different position for yourself. You might think, 'I'm feeling anxious and worried, in short, stressed — this must mean I can't handle my job.' In such thoughts lurks a belief that there is a version of your life available to you that is free from stress. This belief makes us feel less empowered about who we are and what our life should be about, and more overwhelmed with what's going on. As a consequence, you feel not good enough in your job and, at the same time, less likely to be open to talking about your struggles and to seek help. If you define stress in this way, it makes total sense that you would want to avoid it at all costs. Yet, stress is just life tickling you to get your attention. It allows us to experience meaning, to strive for a difference in the world, to make progress towards our goals. Without stress, we wouldn't know what's important and what's not. In other words, stress is an integral part of how we engage with life.

Embracing tension

Professor Kelly McGonigal says that, "Stress is what happens in your body and in your brain when something that you care about is at stake".[144] At such a moment, we activate an immense repertoire of resources to be able to deal with what's coming at us. So, on the positive side, stress is our body and our brain's attempt to help us cope with life as it unfolds, to meet the present moment with adequate preparedness, and to find ways not only to survive, but also thrive. On the negative side, when you feel stressed, you can experience fight, freeze or flight response, and also an array of reactions that go beyond these three.

A common reaction to stress particularly in work-related situation is the 'fawn' response, when you try to please the other person to avoid conflict.[*, 145] When that doesn't work you might experience 'fright' — a feeling of panic, dizziness, nausea, lightheadedness, tingling, and numbing.[146] This is often the moment when we start disassociating from our jobs, our teams and our organisations. If there is still no resolution of the stressful situation, you are likely to progress towards 'flagging', which is the feeling of helplessness, despair and collapse. These are all signals from your parasympathetic nervous system telling you that it is going into shut-down mode. Finally, you might experience the 'faint' response, literally fainting as your body succumbs to a horizontal position to increase blood supply to the brain. Fainting is a physical response in rejection of toxic or poisonous material (be it an actual toxin or a toxic situation).[147]

An alternative path is available to us though. Whenever you become stressed, you can try to react based on your understanding of where you have control and where you don't. That understanding will allow to see that you can reach out to others to help you. To have such *a social response*, some part of you has to recognise that you are not alone in the given situation and that resolving it is not a DIY (Do It Yourself) challenge.[**] When you see this, your brain reacts by realising that you don't have to be alone and then it increases the levels of oxytocin specifically to amp up those social instincts

*   Hence cordial hypocrisy happening so often in politicised organisations. Just to remind you cordial hipocrisy is "the tendency of people in organisations, because of loyalty or fear, to pretend that there is trust when there is none, being polite in the name of harmony when cynicism and distrust are active poisons, eating away at every existence of the organisation".

**   Have you ever found yourself in a situation when you thought that your struggles were only yours, only to find out that other people experience similar struggles as well? This is a crucial element of being able to have *a social response,* I am talking about. For this, you need to allow yourself the vulnerability to share your tension with others around you.

you have to reach out to others.* It gives you the courage and the hope that you need when a job ahead causes you stress. Your mindset is determined by that reaction as your body and brain will always pay attention to your beliefs about yourself in the world, to your narrative. This is what your personal resilience, as a leader, is. Such resilience starts with grit.

Building resilience

Some of us still hold to a false notion that to be a good leader you need talent. Certainly, some people have more inborn qualities that help them on their path to great leadership, but what you truly need is what Dr Angela Duckworth calls *grit*.**, [148] Theodore Roosevelt, the 26th US President, known for his grittiness, spoke about it in his address at the Sorbonne in 1907:

> "It is not the critic who counts; not the man who points out how the strong man stumbles, or where the doer of deeds could have done better. The credit belongs to the man who is actually in the arena, whose face is marred by dust and sweat and blood; who strived valiantly; who errs, who comes again and again, because there is no effort without error and shortcoming; but who does actually strive to do the deeds; who knows great enthusiasms, the great devotions; who spends himself in a worthy cause; who at the best knows in the end the triumph of high achievement, and who at the worst, if he fails, at least fails while daring greatly."

The 32nd US president, Franklin D. Roosevelt, further expanded that notion of grit by saying that, "Courage is not the absence of fear, but rather the assessment that something else is more important than fear".

---

* We associate stress with hormones such as adrenaline and cortisol. What we might not realise is that when we are stressed another hormone is released alongside these: oxytocin. Oxytocin is almost like a chemical of social courage that enables you to face stress and deal with it in a constructive, rather than destructive, way. It provokes you to help others. It also encourages you to let others know that you are struggling and to ask for support.

** Although Merriam-Webster dictionary defines grit as "firmness of character; indomitable spirit", Duckworth proposed a new definition as "perseverance and passion for long-term goals". It it noteworthy that the essence of grit still remains somewhat elusive to many scientists.

You can call yourself gritty if you learn to see failure as learning rather than a sign of your inadequacy. Eleanor Roosevelt (the wife of Franklin D. Roosevelt) completed his statement by giving this simple advice, "Do something that scares you everyday".* This advice is so crucial because grit is like a muscle; it has to be practiced to function well.

To stay courageous and gritty, you need to stay aware of your purpose and vision. These help you to stand in your personal truth and to choose a place from where you thrive. They give you the energy to wake up every morning and deal with the difficulties you might face. Consider the extent to which your purpose and your vision might run your life based on the example of Tom Seaver, an American professional baseball pitcher who played twenty seasons in Major League Baseball.** During his twenty-year long professional career, Seaver aimed to pitch "...the best I possibly can day after day, year after year." He rooted his ambition in his purpose and vision which, in turn, gave meaning and structure to all his daily goals and activities:

> "Pitching... determines what I eat, when I go to bed, what I do when I'm awake. It determines how I spend my life when I'm not pitching. If it means I have to come to Florida and can't get tanned because I might get a burn that would keep me from throwing for a few days, then I never go shirtless in the sun... If it means I have to remind myself to pet dogs with my left hand, then I do that, too. It means in the winter, I eat cottage cheese instead of chocolate chip cookies in order to keep my weight down."***

Purpose and vision frame the context in which you find meaning and value of your long-term efforts, which, in turn, helps you cultivate drive,

---

* The common surname is not coincidental. Theodore Roosevelt was five-times-removed cousin of Franklin Delano Roosevelt and Eleanor Roosevelt was Theodore's niece. So it seems that grit was a family trait.

** Throughout his professional career, Tom Seaver compiled the impressive result of 311 wins, 3640 strikeouts, 61 shutouts and a 2.86 earned run average. In 1992, when Seaver was elected to the Hall of Fame, he received the highest ever percentage of votes: 98.8%.

*** Not to scare you, I might add that such level of determination is required at the absolute pinnacle of sportsmanship. As 'regular' people, we don't have to be that disciplined.

passion and courage. In other words, your purpose and your vision will keep on motivating you to push yourself further and further, regardless of how difficult it may sometimes become.

As a gritty leader you need to be conscientious. Such conscientiousness stems from your integrity towards your purpose and vision, your team, the organisation you are part of — in fact towards the world. Conscientious leaders are concerned about getting a job done in the right way. They are self-disciplined, able to plan rather than forever stay spontaneous, which translates to 'unpredictable' for their peers and business partners. Being conscientious means that you know how to consider possible outcomes and then make decisions leading to results that meet or exceed expectations of those around you.

It also means that you are able to practice compassion and self-compassion. You see what you and others need, then do your best to provide for those needs understanding that, over time, this creates more success for everyone. You know what each person can bring to a project but at the same time you recognise that nobody is perfect and that you are willing to forgive, while making time to teach others how to grow in their roles.

Finally, it means that you have the stamina to follow through. Dr Duckworth writes, "... achievement is the product of talent and effort, the latter a function of the intensity, direction, and duration of one's exertions towards a long-term goal."[149] What she is describing is *deliberate practice* — doing activities to develop specific abilities, identifying weaknesses and working to correct them, and intentionally pushing yourself out of your comfort zone (much like you did in the last twelve weeks).*, **[150][151]

---

*   You might have heard about the rule of 10 000 hours of practice propagated by Malcolm Gladwell in his book *Outliers*.[143] While generally practice is good, it is not the quantity of practice but its quality that matters. Gladwell doesn't differentiate between types of practice. The best way to get better at something is through something known as *deliberate practice*, which is what I am talking about above.

**   Such deliberate practice is best guided by an expert, a skilled coach, or mentor, "someone with an expert eye," according to the author of *Emotional Intelligence*, Daniel Goleman.[144] Coaches and mentors can offer you feedback on specific ways to improve, to develop on your path. They are the first element of your safety net and your support system, which we will further look into in the Outro.

All of these qualities of grit build your resilience as a leader — the ability to get back on the horse after you fall off. Resilience combines optimism (not allowing a moment of failure to ruin your day), with creativity and confidence, which together empower you to reappraise situations and regulate your emotions. Andrew Zolli, the author of *Resilience: Why Things Bounce Back*, beautifully shows how resilience is rooted in your purpose, your ability to influence what's going on and with seeing everything that happens as a learning opportunity.[152]

But above all, your resilience stems from your belief in your own adequacy, your enoughness. It simply means that you understand perfectionism is not something worthwhile striving for in your daily practice as a leader. Perfectionism is pedantic, binary, unforgiving and inflexible. It is focused on an end-game, delivering something in a form that accepts no criticism. This is why those of us who seek perfectionism rarely put anything out there in the world. It is not because their work is not good enough. It is the fear of not satisfying everybody's expectations that stops them from daring to show their work. Marianne Williamson beautifully writes:[153]

Our deepest fear is not that we are inadequate.
Our deepest fear is that we are powerful beyond measure.
It is our light not our darkness that most frightens us.
We ask ourselves, who am I to be brilliant, gorgeous,
talented and fabulous?
Actually, who are you not to be?
You are a child of God.
Your playing small does not serve the world.
There's nothing enlightened about shrinking so that other
people won't feel insecure around you.
We were born to make manifest the glory of
God that is within us.
It's not just in some of us;
it's in everyone.
And as we let our own light shine,
we unconsciously give other people
permission to do the same.
As we are liberated from our own fear,
Our presence automatically liberates others.

What Williamson is demonstrating is that, in a world that is riddled with stress, fast-paced living, unrealistic pursuits of perfection, and a damaging obsession with materialistic wealth, there's an ancient Japanese way of life that can be just what we need right now: the concept of wabi-sabi.

Embracing your leadership wabi-sabi

Wabi-sabi is a worldview that is centred on the acceptance of transience and imperfection.* It means that there is *perfection in imperfection*, and that you forever remain imperfect yourself, even though you keep striving for value (rather than perfection). If you look at the objects that have *wabi-sabi*, they are usually slightly asymmetric, maybe a little rough, definitely simple and intimate. There is within them an appreciation of authenticity and the power of nature.** I strongly believe that, for you as a leader, the ultimate way to deal with stress is to embrace all of your imperfections and see them as your personal asymmetry, roughness and authenticity. If everybody (including you) were predictable and reliable, leadership would just be a matter of ticking boxes on to-do lists. But no-one is perfect so the trick is to find beauty in the imperfections that make you human and to embrace the fact that, although we all strive for excellence, we may never reach it.

Excellence (but not perfection) is the spirit of wabi-sabi. The word 'excellence' stems from the Greek word *arête,* meaning the fulfilment of purpose or function associated with virtue. *Arête* is about forgiving, embracing failure and vulnerability on the ongoing quest for improvement. It allows for disappointment, and prioritises progress over perfection. To paraphrase Tennyson, it is about "...seeking, striving, finding,

---

* Taken individually, *wabi* and *sabi* are two separate concepts. *Wabi* is about recognising beauty in humble simplicity. It invites you to detach from the vanity of materialism so you can experience spiritual richness instead. *Sabi* is concerned with the passage of time, the way all things grow, age, and decay, and how it beautifully manifests itself. It suggests that beauty is hidden beneath the surface of what we actually see, even in what we might perceive as broken.

** We tried to capture the essence of wabi-sabi in the design of this book and especially in the drawings you saw on its pages. Assuredly, they are not pixel-perfect. But aren't they so much more emotionally charged because of their imperfection?

and never yielding".[154] It enables you to see that your notion of excellence develops with you and to understand that today's *enoughness* will be different from tomorrow's, much as it is different from yesterday's.

Growth mindset is the path to your personal and professional wabi-sabi.[155] Growth mindset is about understanding the power of your beliefs (both conscious and unconscious, rational and irrational) and seeing how changing even the simplest of these can have profound impact on nearly every aspect of your life.* Such an approach thrives on challenge and sees failure not as evidence of unintelligence but as a heartening springboard for growth and for stretching your existing abilities. Growth mindset also means that you learn to know how to spend your energy and where you can grow most.

Change your ways and the world will reward you[157]

What I am about to say might sound a little strange for those of you who believe that there is no such thing as coincidence. However, you still might notice that, once you apply the wabi-sabi mindset to your life and work, coincidences start to happen. You might even see them as hard-to-explain synchronicity.

Synchronicity is a concept first proposed by Karl Jung in the 1920s. He wrote, "I found where 'coincidences' which were connected so meaningfully that their 'chance' concurrence would represent a degree of improbability that would have to be expressed by an astronomical figure."**

---

*   In her book *Mindset,* Carol Dweck shows how one of the most basic beliefs we carry about ourselves is our personality. If you find yourself believing that your character, intelligence, or leadership ability is unchangeable, you might be applying a *fixed mindset* attitude towards yourself.[156]

**   Synchronicity has been investigated through the lens of psychology, biology, chaos theory mathematics, and quantum physics. In psychology, it is defined as the occurrence of meaningful coincidences that seem to have no cause; that is, these coincidences are a-causal. In biology, Rupert Sheldrake's work on morphic resonance has principles similar to those of synchronicity. In systems theory, Ernst Lazlo's work on chaos theory has also affirmed the idea of synchronicity. In modern physics, Bohm's work on the holographic cosmos is most consonant with the concept of synchronicity.

According to Jung, this connection is caused by mutual resonance. Many scientists today argue that factors such as confirmation and desirability biases offer a more compelling explanation to synchronicity — people seek out information to support their ideas and ignore information that challenges them (and we are back to the gorilla experiment). There might be an alternative explanation though.

Synchronicity offers an intriguing perspective, where there are answers to our questions everywhere. As long as we hold on to our growth mindset, observe with all our senses and without judgement, and stay open to input and insight from everywhere, meaningful coincidences will occur, which will inspire you to see and do things in new ways and keep on developing on your path. In other words, if we decide to see different things from what we are used to, the 5% of what we used to see may shift and we will notice things we were blind to before.

WEEK

XII

CHALLENGE

Many of us see leadership as hard work. It shouldn't be that hard. There will be difficult days and that's something to embrace. But being a leader is a great place to be and it should feel that way. You just need to find your way to dance with stress to the tune that is comfortable for you. Let's look at some things that can help you see stress for what it is and use it to tend and befriend rather than have it trigger a fight, freeze or flight response.

YOUR EXPERIMENT:
Describe it in three sentences

Your deadline ....

Positive observations	✓	✗	Negative observations
Positive reactions	☺	☹	Negative reactions

Your conclusion ....

What to improve further? ....

CORE TASKS

1. One last time, look at how you organise your day. How have things changed with respect to:

    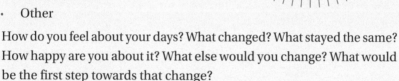

    - Working with strategy
    - Working with people
    - Working with content
    - Education of self and others
    - Enabling and coaching
    - Playing politics
    - Sitting in meetings
    - Evangelising
    - Recuperating
    - Other

    How do you feel about your days? What changed? What stayed the same? How happy are you about it? What else would you change? What would be the first step towards that change?

2. Doing something for the first time leaves a big mark on everyone. The mark is not so big when you do something the second time around. The second time can still be scary but it is scary familiar. You know the moves. You understand the pressure. The unknown becomes known, or at least recognisable.

    Do something for the first time so that you can consciously experience how it feels. Analyse your attitude and emotions towards it.

    I plan to .... for the first time.

    I feel ....

    Check with yourself after you did it.

    - How did I feel right before?
    - How did I feel during?
    - How do I feel now?
    - How might I feel if I were to do it for the second time?

3. Your feelings towards stress can be a complex topic. For once, it is worth seeing it as an indication of the moments that matter. But even if you are able to see this, the question remains: what is your attitude to stress? How can you ensure that your reaction to it will be healthy? How can you take care of yourself physically and psychologically whenever you face a stressful situation?

My attitude towards stress is:
1. ....
2. ....
3. ....
4. ....
5. ....

My attitude towards stress could be improved in the following ways:
1. ....
2. ....
3. ....
4. ....
5. ....

EXTRAS

1. As we are approaching the end of this course I would love to once again say that above all *you* matter — your purpose, your dreams and your humanity. Revisit the topics below and reflect on:
    -   Do I follow my work manifesto? How do I set my boundaries? How can I do it even better?
    -   Who is my sanity committee? How can they help me more?
    -   How do I look for help? Where else could I find it?
    -   How do I make sure I have sufficient slack time? How can I improve on it?
    -   How can I see stress as an indication that a given moment is a moment that matters and see stress as my mind and body helping me rather than consider it as an unwanted guest?

2. Look back at your purpose. How do you feel about it today? Would you like to redefine or perhaps give it more detail? Give it a try.

   My revised purpose is ....

   ....

   ....

3. Look back at the map of your activities (from the Core Task 1). Which of your behaviours do you find self-destructive and which are nurturing? Where do the destructive behaviours come from? Are you still holding onto some irrational behaviours? How can you exhibit more of the nurturing ones and fewer of the destructive ones? How can you root your behaviours more in your purpose?

LOOKING BACK

Here we are, at the very end of your twelve-week journey to define your own leadership. Take a moment to consider what emotions you are experiencing with respect to it and where they come from. How do you see your leadership changed? What are you more confident about now? What is still shaky?

Now, look more specifically back over the previous week:

1. How many core tasks did you manage to complete? How did they help you? Where were you stuck?

2. Did you run your experiment this week? What was it? What was the outcome? Was it noticed by others around you? Is it something you plan to continue with? Or perhaps you have another idea of how to alter and improve on it?

3. What are your preferred tactics of dancing with stress? What else could you add to it?

4. Have you noticed any instances of synchronicity in your life recently? What were they?

5. Was there anything else that resonated with you? What was it? Why do you think it was important? How does it help you define your unique leadership practice?

Outro

Practising self-experimentation
Learning through reflection
Emotional support

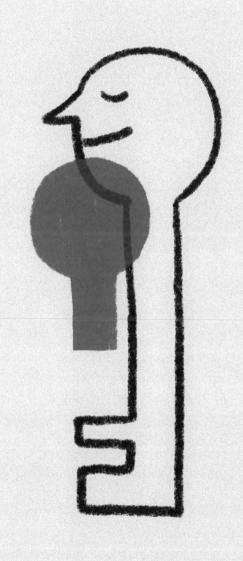

*Congratulations! I hope it feels good to be at this moment
in time. I imagine these past twelve weeks have been rather
intense but I also hope that you can now see significant
change in yourself and your leadership. However, the danger
of going back to the old ways once your practice of self-
reflection and self-experimentation dissipates still lurks.
As we near the end, I would like to invite you to consider
this new leadership practice as your personal apprenticeship
and as access to your private 'leadership gym.'*

First of all, thank you for spending time with this book. I hope it was a journey of discovery, full of personal insights and surprising learnings. I also hope the exercises at the end of each week enabled you to look at yourself and your leadership from many vantage points and on different levels. It was a voyage into your inner world, where your approach was born and then extended out into the external world, where your leadership skills were materialising. The weekly reflection was designed to create the necessary headspace for you to dig deeper to gain new perspectives. It may seem like the end of an adventure but it is only the beginning. You now have an approach and the tools to keep on working on your leadership practice, to apprentice with yourself and with the world around you.

The concept of apprenticeship is typically considered as a practical way for young people to learn a craft. However, if learning is a natural process that occurs via observation, assimilation and emulation over time, apprenticeship should be a life-long process. We can consider ourselves as permanent apprentices in our teams, communities, organisations and contexts. It also means that those around us are in fact our mentors and teachers.

We tend to see mentors as those who are older and more experienced than ourselves. So, as we become mature leaders, it is easy to assume that those who could teach us anything are no longer around. But is that really the case? If we consider everyone as a potential teacher or mentor, things become infinitely more interesting. Some of these mentors may be chosen by you. Some of them will be who I call 'accidental mentors', someone who, for a time, is able to see you clearly and is willing to share with you what they see — the good *and* the bad. Some of these mentors are there for only a short while, some may stay longer. All have a lesson for you that will propel you on your path.

All of them will create for you moments of synchronicity when you will notice more than the 5% of what's going on around you that you usually see.

Consider the youngest person on your team. They can show you how ways of thinking evolve, how communication changes. Your youngest team members help you look anew at the world with optimism, hope and a dose of rebellion — free of both the assumptions and insights you might have. Your peers can mirror your struggles and ways of thinking. And your senior colleagues can share their experiences to inspire you to see a bigger and deeper picture. Isn't it amazing to stay sensitive to all of that?

You can also become your own mentor. Who would be better at that than you? It is especially important since your environment will largely affect your practice. If you are in a start-up organisation you will be a different leader than if you are in a large or mature organisation. You will be a different leader when you are leading a community or if you are a freelancer, inspiring and guiding your clients. It is still you, the very same person, but your leadership practice is likely to be quite different in any of these contexts. As long as you remember that you matter, and that your needs and dreams matter too, you can be your best ally for self-development while always remaining an apprentice of leadership practice.

As you've probably already noticed, once you start changing, the old ways stop working. This is important to keep in mind, otherwise the change might feel scary (even too scary), especially since not everybody will be happy to see the new version of you. There are three elements that can help you stay on your path: self-experimentation, self-reflection and a support system.

Practising self-experimentation

I know I am repeating myself here but let me reiterate this once more. Self-experimentation is about trying out interventions to see if they work, and exploring their effects on your personal behaviour, applicable to your context. The idea is to find interventions that help you achieve your goals in ways that fit your personal preferences, and through this, aid you in establishing sustainable change rather than a temporary fix.

As such, self-experimentation is a quest with no end, guided by your intuition and determined by the environment you find yourself in.

The concept of self-experimentation is built on the assumption that different interventions work differently for every person, which reinforces the premise of this book that there is no one universal leadership model that will work for you (and everybody else). Now, you might be wondering what you should focus on next. As this is your leadership practice and yours only, only you are the best judge of how to proceed. (Though I also hope that by now you have a long list of experiments you want to try, inspired by the various challenges captured during the last twelve weeks). You just need to remember that, as we constantly find ourselves dealing with unpredictable situations in unpredictable environments, we need to acquire deep understanding of how things work for us before we jump into new practices. So, no experimentation makes sense without reflection.

Learning through reflection*

Reflective practice is a way of looking at yourself from an external point of view. You need to ask yourself: *What did I learn about myself, and what works for me and others around me?* Asking this question requires you to calm your mind. It needs time and space. It would be ideal if you could find the time for even the briefest reflection every day, but imagining how busy your days are, I wouldn't be surprised to hear you say it's just too much. My suggestion would be to keep a notebook somewhere within easy reach and write one page as often as possible, but definitely at least once a week.

---

* The philosopher, John Dewey, says that learning through reflection requires three attributes—open-mindedness, responsibility, and wholeheartedness.[158] Open-mindedness can be seen as the ability and desire to hear more than one side of an issue, to give attention to alternative views, and to recognise that even the firmest beliefs may be questioned. Responsibility is the desire to actively search for truth by falsifying rather than confirming your assumptions. Finally, wholeheartedness is an attitude whereby you can overcome fears and uncertainties to make meaningful change and to critically evaluate yourself, your organisation, and your community as to how far they follow through with that change.

Sometimes, you might find yourself resisting reflection as it can become self-judgmental. In such moments, it is important to remember that your beliefs determine the story you tell yourself about the leader you are and want to be. If you sense that your inner critic is taking over, remember that you are just an apprentice in the art of leadership and that every reflection and every experiment is helping you improve. Be gentle with yourself. If you learn that something isn't for you, don't see such an experiment as time wasted. It is in fact a process of exploring your boundaries and your own way of being in the world.

Emotional support

No matter how experienced we are in our roles, we can all feel a little imposter syndrome at times. This feeling is fuelled by the beliefs and narratives we were conditioned by since childhood. These beliefs tell us that we need to fit in by replicating the most common stereotype (eg a female leader must be a warrior, a male leader mustn't show weakness). But it is worth remembering that there is no leadership ideal (much like there is no spoon in the Matrix movie).* You can set your own standard and you have the power to shape it. To retain that power over time, you need emotional support from your peers, your team, your loved ones.

Emotional support increases your resilience and decreases your risk of burnout. But, above all, emotional support creates psychological safety and allows you to experiment and reflect without reinforcing your old habits and non-supportive narratives, especially in challenging situations (often triggered by people who are unhappy with the way you are changing and want you to stay the person you used to be). Be as gentle with them as you are with yourself. Your job is to be in the world in the fullest way possible, but so is theirs. Remember that change takes time, not only for others to adjust to it but, above all, for yourself to understand and implement it. This is the gift of your today's self to your future self. I hope you give it to yourself.

---

*   There are a few things great leaders have in common, such as they stay true to themselves, are not afraid to speak up, take time to think and, maybe most importantly, they know their capabilities, limits and weak spots. Finally, great leaders dare to admit when they are wrong.

Thanks

This book was a strange one to write. First of all, it wanted to emerge as quickly as possible. I have never before experienced such a writing frenzy as I have when writing this book. At the same time, it forced me to face a lot of challenges I have been conveniently hiding from myself. Not everybody liked the change writing this book inspired in me. Some people complained that I became more self-confident and more sure of how I want to be in the world. Some of my relationships changed as a result, some were even broken. But at the end of it, I feel as though I went on a self-pilgrimage through the process of writing, a pilgrimage to discover a person (and a leader) I wanted to be.

I am not a leader in a conventional sense. I don't run a team within an organisation, although I often help teams and their leaders to transition to a state they are happy with. I usually liken it to the hero's journey, with dangers and rising stakes as the hero progresses.[*, 159] I see these journeys as adventures that help those who work with me to discover their best way of doing things.

I envisioned this book more like *The Artist's Way*, maybe not as exciting as the hero's journey from the outside but much more intense on the inside.[161] One possible metaphor is to see it as climbing a mountain, but I am not entirely in favour of that metaphor as it feels finite. I'd rather see it as walking across the mountains. Sometimes you need to climb up, sometimes down, but you always enjoy the views when reaching an area of outstanding beauty. Of course, you will be tired at times but as long as you remain present and take care of yourself, it will remain a joyful journey. I hope it was so for you and that you will continue it beyond this book.

So, first and foremost I would very much like to thank you, my reader — your commitment and your desire to change have brought this book into being. This book is about you and it is yours to interpret and apply. I am merely a signpost on your path to finding your leadership wabi-sabi.

---

*   The hero's journey is a common narrative template that involves a hero who goes on an adventure, learns a lesson, wins a victory with that newfound knowledge, and then returns home transformed.[160]

This book wouldn't have achieved the shape and precision it has without the eagle eye of my ever-supportive husband Łukasz. He combed through every chapter (some of them several times) with the finest tooth-comb to find any inconsistencies and slips of the tongue (or pen). Thank you for being there for me, and happily accepting all the changes that happened within me during my working on this book. I know I am repeating myself but I have to say that — you are the best husband ever!

Malcolm Campbell who wrote the *Foreword* has long been an inspiration for me when it comes to leadership practice. He has the gentle way of leading so needed in today's world. He combines the masculine and the feminine qualities into a graceful mixture of strength and vulnerability. Malcolm, thank you for finding the time for this book.

I would also like to thank Diane Parker, my copyeditor, who enthusiastically responded to my shy enquiry whether she would be willing to edit another book of mine. Your trust in me and my writing, along with your encouragement, were invaluable. Once again, Dominika Wysogląd and Agnieszka Gontarz shaped the look-and-feel of this book. This time they were joined by the extremely talented illustrator Weronika Marianna, who captured the essence of each chapter into visual expression. I can't express how deeply grateful I am for your involvement, enthusiasm and patience. You are the most amazing team any writer could dream of.

I would further very much like to thank BIS Publishers for believing in another project of mine. After reading my proposal, Bionda wrote back, "I went through your proposal, in one breath. And I can be very short about this; Love it!" This is a review any writer dreams about.

I am also grateful to my early readers — Judith Volker, Jessica Mignone, Marcos Cabrera Riande, Steven Thomas and Michael Liehmann. Your comments kept pushing me to go the extra mile to improve this book. I would love to extend special thanks to Rob van der Tillaart who offered me his mentorship, insight and advice for every single chapter. Thank you for your support and encouragement. I would also love to thank Phillip Collins who was there for me as my accountability buddy and my leadership advisor —the sheer speed of writing this book was accelerated by you and the stimulation you offered me.

Thank you!

End Notes

Introduction

1   Tolstoy, L. (1878) *Anna Karenina*. The Russian Messenger.

2   Cameron, J. and Bryan, M., (1993). *The Artist's Way*. Sounds True Recordings.

3   Pressfield, S., (2002). *The War of Art: Break Through the Blocks and Win Your Inner Creative Battles*. Black Irish Entertainment LLC.

4   Rubin, G., (2015). *Better than Before: Mastering the Habits of our Everyday Lives*. Hachette UK

5   Parker-Pope, T. (2021). *To Create a Healthy Habit, Find an Accountability Buddy*. New York Times

WEEK I: Getting Started

6   Kevin Spacey as Frank Underwood in the Netflix drama series *House of Cards*, Season 3, Episode 8, Chapter 34, written by Beau Willimon and directed by John Dahl.

7   Barrett, L.F., (2017). *How Emotions Are Made: The Secret Life Of The Brain*. Pan Macmillan.

8   Barrett, L.F., (2017). *How Emotions Are Made: The Secret Life Of The Brain*. Pan Macmillan.

9   Godin, S. (2015). *Poke the Box: When was the Last Time You Did Something for the First Time?*. Penguin UK.

10   Kahneman, D., Sibony, O. and Sunstein, C.R., (2021). *Noise: A Flaw in Human Judgment*. Little, Brown.

WEEK II: Understanding Your Inner Voice

11   Hurlburt, R. and Schwitzgebel, E., 2011. *Describing Inner Experience?: Proponent Meets Skeptic*. MIT Press.

12   Ellis, A. (1994) *Reason and Emotion in Psychotherapy: Comprehensive Method of Treating Human Disturbances*: Revised and Updated. New York, NY: Citadel Press

13   David, D; Lynn, S. J. & Ellis, A. (2010). *Rational and Irrational Beliefs : Research, Theory, and Clinical Practice*. Oxford University Press.

14   Banks, T., & Zionts, P. (2009). REBT Used With Children And Adolescents Who Have Emotional And Behavioral Disorders In Educational Settings: A Review Of The Literature. *Journal of Rational-Emotive & Cognitive-Behavior Therapy*, 27(1), 51-65.

15   David, D., Lynn, S.J. and Ellis, A. eds., (2010). *Rational and Irrational Beliefs: Research, Theory, and Clinical Practice*. Oxford University Press.

16   Clark, D.A. and Beck, A.T., (2011). *Cognitive Therapy of Anxiety Disorders: Science and Practice*. Guilford Press.

17   Jorn, A. (2016). Rational Emotive Behavior Therapy. *Psych Central*. Retrieved from: https://psychcentral.com/lib/rational-emotive-behavior-therapy/

18   Oltean, H.R., Hyland, P., Vallières, F. and David, D.O., (2017). An Empirical Assessment of REBT Models of Psychopathology and Psychological Health in the Prediction of Anxiety and Depression Symptoms. *Behavioural and Cognitive Psychotherapy*, 45(6), pp.600-615.

19   https://seths.blog/2017/05/emotional-labor/

20   Hochschild, Arlie Russell (1983). *The Managed Heart: Commercialization of Human Feeling*. Berkeley: University of California Press.

21   Hülsheger, U.R.; Schewe, A.F. (2011). On the Costs and Benefits of Emotional Labor: A Meta-analysis of Three Decades of Research. *Journal of Occupational Health Psychology*. 16 (3): 361–389.

22   Grandy, A.; Diefendorff, J.M.; Rupp, D. (2013). *Emotional Labor in the 21st Century: Diverse Perspectives on Emotion Regulation at Work*. Routledge. pp. 3–17.

23   These tasks are inspired by the exercises proposed by the Counselling Centre of the NC State University, which in turn are borrowed from *Tools for Personal Growth* (1999-2010), by James J. Messina, Ph.D. Retrieved from: https://counseling.dasa.ncsu.edu/resources/self-help-resources/irrational-beliefs/

24   Katie, B., (2014). *The Work of Byron Katie*. Eine Einführung.

WEEK III: The Best Version of You

25   James, W., (2007). *The Principles of Psychology* (Vol. 1). Cosimo, Inc..

26   Dehaene, S., (2020). *How We Learn: Why Brains Learn Better Than Any Machine... For Now*. Penguin.

27   Simons, D.J. and Chabris, C.F., (1999). Gorillas in our midst: Sustained inattentional blindness for dynamic events. *Perception*, 28(9), pp.1059-1074.

28   Retrieved from: https://www.youtube.com/watch?v=vJG698U2Mvo

29   Mack, A. and Rock, I., (1998). *Inattentional Blindness*. MIT Press.

30   Frankl, V.E., (1985). *Man's Search for Meaning*. Simon and Schuster.

31   Seligman, M.E.P. (2011). *Flourish: A Visionary New Understanding of Happiness and Well-being*. NY: Free Press

32   Russell, E. and Underwood, C., (2016). Exploring the Role of Purpose in Leadership. *HR Magazine*, pp.46-48.

33   Aftab, A., Lee, E.E., Klaus, F., Daly, R., Wu, T.C., Tu, X., Huege, S. and Jeste, D.V., (2019). Meaning in Life and its Relationship with Physical, Mental, and Cognitive Functioning: a Study of 1,042 Community-dwelling Adults Across the Lifespan. *The Journal of Clinical Psychiatry*, 81(1), pp.0-0.

34   Gravois, J. (2008). You're Not Fooling Anyone. *The Chronicle of Higher Education*, 54(11), A1. Retrieved from http://chronicle.com

35   Sakulku, J., (2011). The Impostor Phenomenon. *Journal of Behavioral Science*, 6(1), pp.75-97.

36   Harvey, J. C., & Katz, C. (1985). *If I'm So Successful, Why do I Feel like a Fake?* New York: Random House.

37   As described by dr Valerie Young, (2011) *The Secret Thoughts of Successful Women: Why Capable People Suffer from the Impostor Syndrome and How to Thrive in Spite of It,* Crown Business NYC.

38   Thompson, T. (2004). Failure Avoidance: Parenting, the Achievement Environment of the Home and Strategies for Reduction. *Learning and Instruction*, 14(1), 3-26.

39   Clance, P. R., Dingman, D., Reviere, S. L., & Stober, D. R. (1995). Impostor Phenomenon in an Interpersonal/Social Context: Origins and Treatment. *Women and Therapy*, 16, 79-96.

40   Clance, P. R., & O'Toole, M. A. (1988). The Impostor Phenomenon: an Internal Barrier to Empowerment and Achievement. *Women and Therapy*, 6(3), 51-64.

41   Clance, P. R., & O'Toole, M. A. (1988). The Impostor Phenomenon: an Internal Barrier to Empowerment and Achievement. *Women and Therapy*, 6(3), 51-64.

42   These insights are drawn from a conversation between Dr Scott Barry Kaufman and Daniel Schmachtenberger based on the podcast episode: "How We Define Creativity". Retrieved from: https://neurohacker.com/define-creativity-dr-scott-barry-kaufman

43   The Ascent Staff. (2019) Study: It Pays to Be Generous, The Ascent. Retrieved from: https://www.fool.com/the-ascent/research/study-it-pays-be-generous

44   Zander, R.S. and Zander, B., (2002). *The Art of Possibility: Transforming Professional and Personal Life*. Penguin.

45 Dehaene, S., (2020). *How We Learn: Why Brains Learn Better Than Any Machine... For Now*. Penguin.

46 Zander, R.S. and Zander, B., (2002). *The Art of Possibility: Transforming Professional and Personal Life*. Penguin.

47 The Big Bang Theory, Season 11, Episode 3 the Relaxation Integration, directed by Chuck Lorry

WEEK IV: Leading With Vision

48 Retrieved from: https://www.cognitive-edge.com/27893-2/

49 Sinek, S., (2019). *The Infinite Game*. Penguin.

50 Carse, J., (2011). *Finite and Infinite Games*. Simon and Schuster.

51 What Are Elon Musk's Ultimate Goals? Overview Of Tesla & SpaceX Plans. (2008) Retrieved from: https://cleantechnica.com/2018/02/17/whats-elon-musks-ultimate-goal-overview-tesla-spacex-plans/.

52 Sinek, S. (2020) *3 Things that Make a MEANINGFUL Vision*. Retrieved from: https://www.youtube.com/watch?v=zpzZumZCdWA

53 Szóstek, A. (2020) The Umami Strategy: Stand Out by Mixing Business with Experience Design. *BIS Publishers*.

54 Levitt, T. (2004). Marketing myopia. *Harvard business review*., *82*(7/8), 138-149.

55 The mapping is inspired by the presentation of Malcolm Campbell at the Agile by Example conference (2019). Retrieved from: https://www.youtube.com/watch?v=wVQAfKNfldk

WEEK V: Expanding Your Worldview

56 Retrieved from: https://haas.berkeley.edu/human-resources/work-life-integration/

57 Covey, S.R., Merrill, A.R. and Merrill, R.R., (1995). *First Things First*. Simon and Schuster.

58 If you'd like to read more about this check out: Dehaene, S., (2020). *How We Learn: Why Brains Learn Better Than Any Machine... For Now*. Penguin, p. 89.

59 Viswanathan, P. and Nieder, A., (2015). Differential Impact of Behavioral Relevance on Quantity Coding in Primate Frontal and Parietal Neurones. *Current Biology*, *25*(10), pp.1259-1269.

60 Dehaene, S., (2020). *How We Learn: Why Brains Learn Better Than Any Machine... For Now*. Penguin, p. 159.

61   Amalric, M., Wang, L., Pica, P., Figueira, S., Sigman, M. and Dehaene, S., (2017). The Language of Geometry: Fast Comprehension of Geometrical Primitives and Rules in Human Adults and Preschoolers. *PLoS Computational Biology*, *13*(1), p.e1005273.

62   Ferriss, T. (2017). *Tools of Titans: The Tactics, Routines, and Habits of Billionaires, Icons, and World-Class Performers.* Houghton Mifflin.

63   Karl, J.A. and Fischer, R., (2018). Rituals, Repetitiveness and Cognitive Load. *Human Nature, 29*(4), pp.418-441.

64   Retrieved from: https://www.youtube.com/watch?v=35sp4S2w9ZI

65   Allen, D., (2015). *Getting Things Done: the Art of Stress-free Productivity.* Penguin.

66   Janis, I. L. (1972). *Victims of Groupthink: A Psychological Study of Foreign-policy Decisions and Fiascoes.* Haughton Mifflin.

67   Janis, I.L., (2008). Groupthink. *IEEE Engineering Management Review*, 36(1), p.36.

68   Tetlock, P.E. and Gardner, D., (2016). *Superforecasting: The Art and Science of Prediction.* Random House.

69   Surowiecki, J., (2005). *The Wisdom of Crowds.* Anchor.

70   Tetlock, P.E. and Gardner, D., (2016). *Superforecasting: The Art and Science of Prediction.* Random House.

71   Janis, I. L. (1972). *Victims of Groupthink: A Psychological Study of Foreign-policy Decisions and Fiascoes.* Haughton Mifflin.

72   Janis, I. L. (1972). *Victims of Groupthink: A Psychological Study of Foreign-policy Decisions and Fiascoes.* Haughton Mifflin.

73   Aristotle: *Politics* III.1281b. Translated by H. Rackham, Loeb Classical Library

74   De Bono, E., (2017). *Six Thinking Hats.* Penguin.

75   Retrieved from: https://www.catchingthenextwavepodcast.com/episodes/806-yuan-wang

76   Brown, B., (2021). *Atlas of the Heart: Mapping Meaningful Connection and the Language of Human Experience.* Ebury Publishing

77   Bloom, P., (2017). *Against Empathy: The Case for Rational Compassion.* Random House.

78   Taylor, Steve (Sep 12, 2015) *Understanding Empathy: Shallow and Deep Empathy.* Psychology Today. Retrieved from: https://www.psychologytoday.com/us/blog/out-the-darkness/201509/understanding-empathy

79   Small, D.A. and Loewenstein, G., (2003). Helping a Victim or Helping the Victim: Altruism and Identifiability. *Journal of Risk and uncertainty*, *26*(1), pp.5-16.

80   Bruneau, E. G., Cikara, M., & Saxe, R. (2017). Parochial Empathy Predicts Reduced Altruism And The Endorsement Of Passive Harm. *Social Psychological and Personality Science, 8*(8), 934-942.

WEEK VII: Building Trust

81   Calvo, R.A. and Peters, D., (2014). *Positive Computing: Technology for Well-being and Human Potential.* MIT Press.

82   Goetz, J.L., Keltner, D., and Simon-Thomas, E. (2010). Compassion: an Evolutionary Analysis and Empirical Review. *Psychological Bulletin 136*, 3, 351.

83   Flynn, J.R. and Flynn, J.R., (2012). *Are We Getting Smarter?: Rising IQ in the Twenty-first Century.* Cambridge University Press.

84   Barrett, L.F. (2020). *Seven and a Half Lessons About The Brain.* Picador.

85   Machiavelli, Niccolo. "The Prince (1513)." *Hertfordshire: Wordsworth Editions* (1993).

86   Solomon, R. C., & Flores, F. (2003). *Building Trust: In Business, Politics, Relationships, and Life.* Oxford University Press.

87   Mills, A.K. (2016). *Everyone is a Change Agent.* Engine for Change Press.

88   Mills, A.K. (2016). Everyone is a Change Agent. Engine for Change Press.

89   Lewicki, R.J., McAllister, D.J. and Bies, R.J., (1998). Trust and Distrust: New Relationships and Realities. *Academy of Management Review, 23*(3), pp.438-458.

90   Hofstede, G., (2011). Dimensionalizing Cultures: the Hofstede Model in Context. *Online Readings in Psychology and Culture, 2*(1), pp.2307-0919.

91   Luhmann, N., (2018). *Trust and Power.* John Wiley & Sons.

92   Liz Ryan, Ten Ways To Build Trust On Your Team, *Forbes*, March 17, 2018. Retrieved from: https://www.forbes.com/sites/lizryan/2018/03/17/ten-ways-to-build-trust-on-your-team/?sh=7238cd7b2445

93   Whitener, E.M., Brodt, S.E., Korsgaard, M.A. and Werner, J.M., (1998). Managers as Initiators of Trust: an Exchange Relationship Framework for Understanding Managerial Trustworthy Behavior. *Academy of Management Review, 23*(3), pp.513-530.

94   Godin S.,(2017) Let's Stop Calling Them 'Soft Skills': They Might Be Skills, But They're Not Soft. *Published on Medium.* Retrieved from: https://medium.com/its-your-turn/ lets-stop-calling-them-soft-skills-9cc27ec09ecb.)

WEEK VIII: Daring To Dare

95   Retrieved from: https://quoteinvestigator.com/2018/11/18/know-trouble/

96   As proposed by Philip Tetlock and described by Grant, A., (2021). *Think Again: The Power of Knowing What You Don't Know*. Viking.

97   Grant, A., (2021). *Think Again: The Power of Knowing What You Don't Know*. Viking.

98   Tetlock, P.E. and Gardner, D., (2016). *Superforecasting: The Art and Science of Prediction*. Random House.

99   Grant, A., (2021). *Think Again: The Power of Knowing What You Don't Know*. Viking.

100   Feynman, R.P., (2009). *The Meaning Of It All: Thoughts Of A Citizen-Scientist*. Basic Books.

101   Feynman, R. P., & Sackett, P. D. (1985). "Surely You're Joking Mr. Feynman!"Adventures of a Curious Character. *American Journal of Physics*, *53*(12), 1214-1216.

102   Chernyshenko, O.S., Kankaraš, M. and Drasgow, F., (2018). Social and Emotional Skills for Student Success and Well-being: Conceptual Framework for the OECD Study on Social and Emotional Skills.

103   Dehaene, S., (2020). *How we Learn: Why Brains Learn Better than Any Machine... for Now*. Penguin.

104   *Metaphysics* I.2

105   Dweck, C., (2017). *Mindset: Changing the Way You Think to Fulfil Your Potential* (updated edition). Hachette UK.

106   Edmondson, A., (1999). Psychological Safety and Learning Behavior in Work Teams. *Administrative Science Quarterly*, 44(2), pp.350-383.

107   Fredrickson, B.L., (2000). Why Positive Emotions Matter in Organizations: Lessons from the Broaden-and-Build Model. *Psychologist-Manager Journal*, 4(2), p.131.

108   Rozovsky, J., (2015) The Five Keys To A Successful Google Team. Rework. Retrieved from: https://rework.withgoogle.com/blog/five-keys-to-a-successful-google-team

109   Delizonna, L., (2015) *Mindful Leaders: A Self-Coaching Guide & Toolkit*. Createspace Independent Publishing Platform.

110   Retrieved from: https://seths.blog/2011/08/the-warning-signs-of-defending-the-status-quo/

111   Mills, A.K. (2016). *Everyone is a Change Agent*. Engine for Change Press.

WEEK IX: Developing Infinite Relationships

112 Carse, J. (2011). *Finite and Infinite Games*. Simon and Schuster.

113 Kubota, J.T., Banaji, M.R. and Phelps, E.A. (2012). The Neuroscience of Race. *Nature Neuroscience, 15*(7), pp.940-948.

114 Todd, A.R., Thiem, K.C. and Neel, R. (2016). Does Seeing Faces of Young Black Boys Facilitate the Identification of Threatening Stimuli? *Psychological Science, 27*(3), pp.384-393.

115 Zander, R.S. and Zander, B. (2002). *The Art of Possibility: Transforming Professional and Personal Life*. London: Penguin.

116 Barrett, L.F. (2020). *Seven and a Half Lessons about the Brain*. Boston: Houghton Mifflin Harcourt.

117 Gottman, J.M. and Levenson, R.W. (2000). The Timing of Divorce: Predicting When a Couple will Divorce over a 14-year Period. *Journal of Marriage and Family*, 62 (3), pp.737–745.

118 Gladwell, M. (2000). *The Tipping Point: How Little Things Can Make a Big Difference*. Little, Brown and Company.

119 T. Erickson, Ch. Halverson, W. A. Kellogg, M. Laff, and T. Wolf. (2002). Social Translucence: Designing Social Infrastructures That Make Collective Activity Visible. *Communications of ACM*, 45(4):40–44.

120 Stone, D. and Heen, S. (2015). *Thanks for the Feedback: the Science and Art of Receiving Feedback Well (Even When it is Off Base, Unfair, Poorly Delivered, and Frankly, You're Not in the Mood)*. Penguin.

121 Mills A. K. (2021). *Change Tactics: 50 Ways Change Agents Boldly Escape the Status Quo*. Engine For Change Press.

122 Retrieved from: https://www.gallup.com/workplace/236951/praise-praising-employees.aspx

123 Owens, B.P., Rowatt, W.C. and Wilkins, A.L., (2011). Exploring The Relevance And Implications Of Humility In Organizations. *Handbook of Positive Organizational Scholarship*, pp.260-272.

WEEK X: Making Decisions

124 Retrieved from: https://seths.blog/2017/12/choosing-with-out-deciding/

125 Kubler-Ross, E., (1969) *On Death and Dying*, Macmillan, NY.

126 Allan, J.L., Johnston, D.W., Powell, D.J., Farquharson, B., Jones, M.C., Leckie, G. and Johnston, M. (2019). Clinical Decisions and Time Since Rest Break: An Analysis of Decision Fatigue in Nurses. *Health Psychology, 38*(4), p.318.

127 Gilbert, E. (2015). Big Magic: How To Live a Creative Life, And Let Go Of Your Fear. Bloomsbury Publishing.

128   Retrieved from: https://seths.blog/2021/05/
       sunk-costs-creativity-and-your-practice/

129   Schwartz, B., (2004), *The Paradox of Choice: Why More is Less.* Ecco.

130   Jaffé, M. E., Reutner, L., & Greifeneder, R. (2019). Catalyzing decisions: How
       a coin flip strengthens affective reactions. *Plos One, 14*(8), e0220736.

WEEK XI: Becoming an Influencer

131   Pink, D.H. (2013). *To Sell is Human: The Surprising Truth about Moving
       Others.* Penguin.

132   Vogler, C. (2007). *The Writer's Journey.* Studio City, CA: Michael Wiese
       Productions.

133   General Stanley McChrystal. *Mastering Risk: A User's Guide.* Tim Fer-
       riss Show, Episode 535, September 30, 2021. Retrieved from: https://tim.
       blog/2021/09/30/general-stanley-mcchrystal/

134   Clark, H. (1996) *Using Language* (Volume 1). Cambridge University Press,
       New York, 1st edition.

135   Goffman, E. (1967). *Interaction Ritual: Essays in Face-to-face Behavior.*
       Random House Inc.

136   Pink, D.H. (2013). *To Sell is Human: the Surprising Truth about Moving
       Others.* Penguin.

137   Stanier, M.B. (2016). *The Coaching Habit: Say Less, Ask More & Change
       the Way you Lead Forever.* Box of Crayons Press.

138   Nutt, P.C. (2003). *Why Decisions Fail: Avoiding the Blunders and Traps
       that Lead to Debacles.*

139   Stanier, M.B. (2016). *The Coaching Habit: Say Less, Ask More & Change
       the Way you Lead Forever.* Box of Crayons Press.

140   Gaver, B. and Martin, H. (2000). Alternatives: Exploring Information Appli-
       ances Through Conceptual Design Proposals. In *Proceedings of the SIGCHI
       Conference on Human Factors in Computing Systems*, pp. 209–216.

141   Sweller, J. (April 1988). Cognitive Load During Problem Solving: Effects on
       Learning. *Cognitive Science.* 12 (2): 257–285.

142   Schwartz, B. (2004). *The Paradox of Choice: Why More is Less.* New York:
       Ecco.

143   Pink, D.H. (2013). *To Sell is Human: The Surprising Truth about Moving
       Others.* Penguin.

144   Retrieved from: https://yourstudioe.com/blog/upside-of-stress/

WEEK XII: Your Leadership Wabi-Sabi

145   Walker, P. (2018). *Complex PTSD: From Surviving to Thriving.* Tantor Audio.

146   Schauer, E. and Elbert, T. (2010). The Psychological Impact of Child Sol-
      diering. In *Trauma Rehabilitation After War and Conflict* (pp. 311-360).
      Springer, New York, NY.

147   Schauer, E. and Elbert, T. (2010). *Trauma Rehabilitation after War and
      Conflict: Community and Individual Perspectives.*

148   Duckworth, A. (2016). *Grit: The Power of Passion and Perseverance* (Vol.
      234). New York, NY: Scribner.

149   Duckworth, A. (2016). *Grit: The Power of Passion and Perseverance* (Vol.
      234). New York, NY: Scribner.

150   Gladwell, M. (2016). *Outliers.* Mediacat Yayıncılık.

151   Goleman, D. (1995). *Emotional Intelligence.* New York: Bantam Books

152   Zolli, A. and Healy, A.M. (2012). *Resilience: Why Things Bounce Back.*
      Hachette UK.

153   Williamson, M. and Williamson, M. (2005). *A Return to Love.* Harper Collins
      Publishers.

154   Tennyson, Alfred Tennyson, Baron (1809-1892). *Poems. Ulysses.* Everyman,
      2004.

155   Dweck, C. (2017). *Mindset (updated edition): Changing The Way You Think
      To Fulfil Your Potential.* Hachette UK.

156   Dweck, C. (2017). Mindset – Updated Edition: *Changing The Way You Think
      To Fulfil Your Potential.* Hachette UK.

157   Adams D. (1987). *Dirk Gently's Holistic Detective Agency.* William Heine-
      mann Ltd. UK.

158   Dewey, J., 1997. *How We Think.* Courier Corporation.

Thanks

159   Campbell, J. (2008). *The Hero With a Thousand Faces* (Vol. 17). New World
      Library.

160   Campbell, J. (2008). The Hero With A Thousand Faces (Vol. 17). New World
      Library.

161   Cameron, J. and Bryan, M. (1993). *The Artist's Way.* Sounds True Recordings.